FINDING
the FATHER

IN THE STORY OF
THE CHURCH

Trevor Galpin

Published by TLG Mins

First Published in Great Britain in 2016.

Cover design by Tom Carroll

British Library Cataloguing in Publication Data

ISBN: 978-0-9575318-4-0

Contents

Preface

I started thinking about writing this book because a number of times I have been asked to teach a short course on the story of the church through 2000 years. I have been interested in Church History since my days in college. I had been inspired to study Church History by my tutor, Dr. Raymond Brown, then principal of Spurgeon's College in London, UK. He loved the subject and it rubbed off. My short course inevitably was superficial and subjective simply because there was so much to include and a large amount to exclude. Therefore, I tried to paint a big picture rather than a detailed account.

People started asking me for copies of my notes. I had notes that were not very readable. Also my notes were to be used as prompts and therefore spoken and taught rather than read. They had been collected over the years from all sorts of books and sources and it was very hard to say where I had picked up the information. It was clear I needed to tidy things up and present this material in a more readable format. One of my aims when I taught also applies to this book, it was to inspire the reader to dig further and explore the rich wells of the story of the Church. As a result, I have not written an academic scholarly work and by that I mean it is not full of detailed footnotes like a theological or historical treatise. Instead, I have written a story. Where I have referenced something it is primarily to acknowledge the source of a major quotation or a book or author whose influence has been significant to me.

Some people struggle with the very idea of reading history. Famously,

Henry Ford the founder of the Ford Motor Company in the USA writing in the Chicago Tribune in 1916 said, "History is more or less bunk. It's tradition. We don't want tradition. We want to live in the present, and the only history that is worth a tinkers damn is the history that we make today."

I profoundly disagree with that statement. Christianity is a historical religion. God has revealed himself in and through history. The Old Testament is a historical revelation of God at work through his relationship with his people. God does not reveal himself through doctrinal statements but through his relationship and interactions with his people through the ages. In the Old Testament, he instructed people to tell the stories of his dealings with them to their children and then their children.

The great Roman orator, Cicero in the first century BC said that to not know what took place before you were born was to remain forever a child. To have no memory of the past is a serious psychiatric or mental condition. We do all we can to help people to recover their memories. A community with no social memory is suffering a serious illness.

What is history? It is a collection of stories, memories, and writings from all sorts of perspectives. Much is a subjective description of past events by people commenting on what they witnessed from their personal perspective. Sometimes what they have recorded was a description of someone they didn't like or who didn't think in the same way as they did, effectively their enemy! Impartiality, as a result, was easily lost.

Sometimes history is gleaned from objects, inscriptions, paintings and artefacts from the past that need to be interpreted. Historians build a picture of what they think happened in the past by studying these things. We are very dependent on those whose passion is to describe the events from the past, the historians, theologians and writers who have made the study of the past their life's work. Increasingly, I am seeing that this whole process is very, very subjective. I don't think this book will be very different.

However, as I looked at the story of the church, I began to see that it was not just a story. It was not just memories. I began to see very clearly that the story was one of incredible depth and the unfolding of an amazing revelation. I began to see that the early church lost touch with its beginnings and the Church evolved into a vast multifaceted worldwide organisation made up of thousands of varying expressions very different from its original form. Specifically, I saw that there was a steady loss of key biblical truth generation after generation over many centuries. Equally, in time there was a restoration of key biblical truth that God has graciously given back to the Church particularly over the last five hundred years. As a result, this book became a charting of this process. My particular interest in this is because in many ways it has reflected my own journey of rediscovery culminating in the amazing awakening within me of knowing the triune God not just as Jesus my saviour, the Holy Spirit my comforter but also as God my Father.

In short, the purpose of this book is to try to follow how the revelation of the Father that Jesus brought and that is recorded in the New Testament gradually began to be lost by succeeding generations of Christian writers and teachers and was then given back or restored to the church. This loss was slow, but sadly constant from the late first century to the Middle Ages. Then, from the sixteenth century onward, there was equally a steady rediscovery of the three persons of the Trinity: first Jesus, then the Holy Spirit, culminating in the present day revelation of God the Father and our resulting identity as sons.

This book is therefore more about the development historically of theological truth than just church history. However, the two are deeply connected. To understand the development of theological truth, we need to see where this sits within the big picture of history. Many have heard bits and pieces of the story and know about some sections, so what I have tried to do in this book is join the dots. For many, the story of the church is a jumble of isolated events and people who are not connected, rather like the pieces of a jigsaw puzzle. The reality is that there is a flow to the story, a pulsing of the Holy Spirit as he energizes the people of God in every generation to seek for truth even when all around them there is corruption and stagnation in the Church. The puzzle is actually a magnificent picture!

God's work in history is a secret work, a mystery even. At times, it is an exciting and happy story, full of joy. Other times, it is downright dreadful and humiliating when it is very difficult to see the finger of God in the process. For example, how on earth could Christians read that Jesus told us to "love your enemies" then think it was still okay to burn them at the stake. Beats me.

Sometimes, the story reads in such soiled and earthy terms as to make us question 'Where was God?' It's easy to see him in Athanasius, Francis of Assisi, the Great Awakening, in revivals and Mother Theresa, but more difficult to find him in the Viking onslaught that wiped out the Celtic Church, in the Crusades and in Auschwitz. In the story, while there is great sadness and darkness there were always moments of great light. There were people who held high the light of the gospel of truth and revelation when all around was very dark.

The great tapestry that is the story of the Church is woven with dark threads as well as bright silken threads. This book is not about the 'whys' of history, though I have my opinions that will inevitably pop out. Rather, it is about the wheat and the weeds growing up together alongside each other as in Jesus' parable in Matthew 13:24. In the end, the harvest of the wheat is gathered in despite the weeds. We do know how the story ends in so far as it ends for us in the early twenty-first century. Though as C.S. Lewis supposedly said if Jesus does not return in the next two thousand years, they will look back at our era as still being in the Early Church.

So on with the story...

CHAPTER ONE

The New Testament Era

In the middle of the first century AD, Paul the Apostle wrote in what was most likely his first letter,

> *"In the fullness of time God sent forth his Son."*
> *Galatians 4:4*

This was about a new day of revelation and visitation in which God began to speak clearly to us about his nature and his desire for relationship with us as his sons and daughters. Paul was announcing that God had sent his Son. The silence of centuries was over. The writer to the Hebrews says in his introduction,

> *"In the past God spoke to our ancestors through the prophets at many times and in various ways, but in these last days he has spoken to us by his Son, whom he appointed heir of all things, and through whom also he made the universe."*
> HEBREWS 1:1-2

More than four hundred years had passed since the close of the Old Testament. During those years no word had been received by anyone recognised by the community of Israel as a prophet. The last word that God had spoken was through the prophet Malachi,

> *"See, I will send the prophet Elijah to you before that great and dreadful day of the Lord comes. He will turn the hearts of the parents to their children, and the hearts of the children to their parents."*
>
> - MALACHI 4:5-6A

The people of God were waiting for the Messiah to come and God had said that another "Elijah" would precede him. However, they did not know that he would be God's Son! The revelation that the Messiah brought was that Yahweh, the Almighty God was our true Father and that he, Jesus himself is his son. He was to be the one who would end the separation between mankind and God that had existed since the fall of Adam. Jesus would be the one who would send the Holy Spirit to pour the love of the Father into the hearts of all those who received him.

THE FIRST CENTURY WORLD

Jesus was born around 6 BC in the city of Bethlehem, in the region of Judea, the territory of the Jewish king, Herod, a king who owed his throne to the Romans. At that time, there were three huge factors all working together that would aid the spread of this message that Jesus came to reveal: Greek culture, the Jewish world and the Roman empire.

Jesus' world was dominated by the Roman Empire. The majority of the people within the empire spoke and thought like Greeks.

Since the capture of the kingdom of Israel by the Assyrians, the fall of the Kingdom of Judah and the destruction of the city of Jerusalem by the Babylonians two centuries later, the Jews had been scattered across the known world. This scattering came to be known as the Jewish Diaspora or dispersion.

The survival of the Jews as a recognisable group was primarily because of their religion. Jewish religion was a religion of a book based firmly on the Law of Moses, the Torah, which consists of the first five books of the Old Testament. Judaism in the first century was not confined to Palestine. It had spread all over the Roman world and beyond to the east in the old lands of the Assyrians, the Babylonians and their conquerors the Persians and then their conquerors the Greeks. Their book, the Torah, had gone with them into exile and in Alexandria in Egypt seventy Jewish scholars had undertaken a translation of the Old Testament into Greek. This had been completed about two hundred years before the coming of Jesus. This translation was called the Septuagint after the seventy scholars and when abbreviated is referred to as 'LXX'. All the Jews across the Diaspora used this translation and it was 'the Scriptures' used by the early church. When Paul said that, *"All Scripture is inspired by God and useful"* (2 Tim 3:16) this is probably what he had in mind along with the original Hebrew version that he would have known as a Pharisee.

The Jews were doctrinally convinced monotheists. They believed in one true God who they knew as 'Yahweh'. The Jews were too afraid to call God by his name. Instead, they called him 'Adonai', the LORD. This monotheistic view contrasted with the pagan world-view of everyone else around them who believed in multiple gods. For the Jews, God was a moral being, whereas they viewed the pagan gods as basically immoral. Judaism taught a loving purpose of God that was concentrated in the Messiah who would come and establish a theocracy in Israel with its centre being Jerusalem. This is where the LORD would re-establish a kingdom in Israel and from where the Messiah would rule as king. The Greek word for this Messiah was Christos, the Christ or the anointed one. They did not have any concept that the Messiah would be the divine Son of God. They did not even know that God had a son.

When they lost their king and independence in the sixth century BC, Judaism became a scattered spiritual community centred around the 'synagogue'. The synagogue was a gathering together of Jews and not primarily a building. Ten male Jews in a community constituted a synagogue and eventually, purpose built structures were erected to house this group. As a result, there were synagogues in all principal cities across the empire. In larger cities, such as Rome, Alexandria and Antioch, there were many synagogues. Alexandria had a huge Jewish colony that at its height had hundreds of thousands of Jews.

The Jews were geographically scattered throughout the Roman Empire. It is estimated that about 7% of the empire's population was Jewish. Like most parts of the empire, these Jewish colonies had become Greek speaking.

The Romans treated Jews, unlike other religious groups and cultures with special favour. They were free to live according to their own traditions and laws and were exempt from military service. They were excused participation in the Imperial Cult or Roman Religion but as a result were socially despised as a race set apart. They were not approved of by the majority and considered objects of vulgar distrust, despised by most people. The Roman historian Tacitus had nothing good to say about them. In Book Five, section 5 of *The Histories* by Tacitus, he writes, "*The Jews regard as profane all that we hold sacred and permit all that we abhor.*"

Since the conquests of the Macedonian king, Alexander the Great in the fourth century BC, the culture of Greece had spread throughout the Mediterranean world and beyond into the east. Greek language and culture became fashionable for all educated people and was spoken all over the Empire. The language of trade, business, education and the streets in the first century was Greek. It is referred to as 'Koine' Greek and is simpler than the classical Greek of the previous centuries. It was the 'lingua franca' of the Roman world. All of the New Testament was written in Koine Greek. It was the language of the people. Greek religion was widespread and Greek philosophy was said to have taught the Roman world how to think. Along with this, there was a search for truth that gave people an inquiring spirit which spread all over the Empire among the educated upper classes and filtered down to most ordinary people.

The apostle Paul was typical of his time. He grew up in Tarsus, a major Greek trade centre and university city. Tarsus was a centre of Stoic philosophy and in his letters, Paul drew from his knowledge of Stoic philosophy, occasionally using Stoic terms and metaphors to assist his new Gentile converts in their understanding of the revelation of God. In his sermon to the Greek audience in Athens recorded in Acts 17, he quoted from a number of Greek philosophers and poets.

However, there was widespread immorality within the Greek culture and this had also permeated throughout society. There was a very low value put on human life. Slavery was everywhere and at one time it was thought that 90% of the Roman world might have been slaves. Amongst many there was a longing for a force to reform men's character and as a result a number of Greek speakers began to embrace Jewish thinking.

Following the civil wars, in 31 BC, after the assassination of dictator

Julius Caesar, there had been peace throughout the Roman Empire when Octavius Caesar was declared the Emperor Augustus. Rome remained at peace until the end of second century AD. There were a few minor uprisings, not least in Judea in AD 70 that resulted in the destruction of the temple and the end of the Jewish state. Generally, the Empire was to enjoy two hundred years of ease of movement and comparative peace. This is known as the Pax Romana, the Roman Peace. This period of stability aided the spread of Christianity immensely. Throughout the Empire, many nations and tribes were brought together. Greek became the common language of government, commerce and education. Citizenship was extended to suitable people and highly coveted by aspiring peoples. The apostle Paul was a Roman citizen. According to the Book of Acts, he inherited Roman citizenship from his father who had also been a Pharisee. As a Roman citizen, he also bore the Latin name of "Paul". He used his rights as a citizen to give him freedom of movement and when on trial, he appealed to the Emperor in Rome to be tried there rather than remain in Judea for his impending trial.

The spread of commerce, economic activity and trade accompanied the Roman peace. The road network was safe and fast. It was possible to travel from Jerusalem to Rome in just weeks by ship and a couple of months by road. Pirate fleets had been attacked and neutralised by the Roman navy and this aided safety in seafaring. Postal services were advanced and widely used throughout the empire. Letters and messages were quickly delivered. The New Testament is full of letters from the first century. New ideas travelled very quickly as a result.

Roman Religion was a state religion that included a belief in the divinity of the Emperor alongside all the ancient gods of Rome. The emperor was the head of state, the army and religion. The Romans were tolerant of other religions and gods and adopted them into their own religious pantheon as long as people believed in the new Roman gods. Particularly, the divinity of the emperor. To prove loyalty to the emperor all that was required was to swear to the divinity of the emperor by saying 'Caesar is Lord.'

These three major influences all contributed to the rapid and early spread of the Christian message. The early church that became established in the first century was initially founded in a Jewish community, speaking Greek and living in the Roman Empire. All these factors influenced the beginnings of the new community who called themselves the 'Followers of the Way'.

Many have been amazed at the way the early church so quickly established itself and began to spread across the Roman world. Within a very few years, there were Christian groups in nearly all the major cities of the eastern part of the Roman Empire and even in the capital Rome itself.

Indeed, in the fullness of time God sent his Son.

FOLLOWERS OF THE WAY

But what did these followers of the Way believe? What had they discovered that was so radical and unique? What was so special and life changing about this new revelation that so captivated peoplevelationthat wminds that they were willing to die for their newfound beliefs? Where do we begin to discover this truth about God who is Spirit revealed as a Father through his Son?

In seeking how the revelation of God as our Father and our status as sons has been revealed to us, we need to look carefully at the New Testament. The starting point has to be the New Testament because its writers were the first witnesses, the carriers of this revelation. They were the ones who brought it to the world. It is these writings that contain the revealed truth about the nature of God that would survive the scrutiny of every generation since right up to the present day. It is within the pages of the New Testament that we discover just who God is and how he has revealed himself to us as a Father. The writers of the New Testament were building on a revelation that they had found implicitly in the Old Testament. Yet their understanding they received goes far beyond the teaching of the Old Testament.

When we open up the New Testament, we immediately notice a number of things. The first is that it is a collection of various documents that include historical and biographical narratives, letters to churches and individuals and the last book, an apocalyptic vision of the future. The second thing we notice is that these types of material are not arranged chronologically rather they are grouped together according to type and authorship. So the first five books are broadly speaking historical narratives, the four gospels and the Acts of the Apostles. These are followed by a group of letters attributed to the Apostle Paul. Following these come a group of general letters written by various people and finally, unique to the New Testament, an apocalyptic writing we know as the Revelation of John.

Popular Christianity has used the New Testament rather like a supermarket of truth that we dip into on a regular basis looking for our favourite bits. Sometimes we hang out in the Gospel aisle and ignore the meat section of Paul's letters. On occasions, we visit the intoxicating liquor aisle of Revelation. Whilst we know there is a big picture here, we tend to look at the detail and miss sometimes the grand scope of the overall picture.

Many have written extensively on each of the New Testament documents, exploring their authorship, when they were written, their structure, language and content. That is not the scope of this work. I am looking for a thread, a river that runs through the New Testament, an even greater truth than the individual sections contain about the revelation of God as Father. To do that, I have adopted a chronological approach to see what happened first if that is possible.

THE ACTS OF THE APOSTLES

Historical detail is found in the four Gospels, The Acts of the Apostles and in some of the Letters of Paul but these were not written at the same time. So where do we begin? Whilst it may not have been the earliest document written, the Acts of the Apostles describes the events of the beginnings of the church mainly from the viewpoint of eyewitnesses. It is of course Luke's second volume and follows on from his first, which is his Gospel. Like the Gospels, we have eyewitness accounts of many of the events Acts describes. I have written extensively about this in my book, *Jesus and his Father.*

The book known as Acts begins with what happened after a man they thought was dead was found walking around in a graveyard! It is all about Jesus who had been raised from the dead. When we read our Bibles in their current format we are not unreasonably surprised that following the huge emphasis on the revelation by Jesus of God being his Father in the Gospels, there is next to nothing in the early chapters of Acts to support or reinforce that revelation. It is as if the early church did not have that revelation! So what is happening in Acts and why is there apparently so little about what is clearly a major theme of the Gospels, especially John's Gospel?

Luke, who was a travelling companion of Paul, wrote Acts. He was present at some of the events that are described in the later part of the book and was an eyewitness of much of what he writes about. The Gospels may not been written until about the year 60 at the earliest so Luke's account of Acts gives us invaluable information of how the Early Church began and developed even though he wrote it after he had written his gospel. There are also important clues scattered throughout Paul's letters about people and the churches that he had planted and related to.

The Acts of the Apostles describes the beginnings of the church in Jerusalem that was essentially a Jewish church. In Acts chapters 1 – 7, the activity took place in and around Jerusalem. Then the church began to touch the Gentile world in Acts chapters 8 – 12 as the Apostles encountered Gentiles such as Cornelius the Roman centurion and the Ethiopian eunuch. The church also began to face persecution in which Stephen, one of the leaders in Jerusalem, was stoned to death (Acts 6:6–60). Later, James the son of Zebedee, Jesus' cousin, was the first of the Apostles to be martyred (Acts 12:1-3).

Paul's conversion is recorded in Acts chapter 9, and his first missionary journey in chapters 13 – 14.

Simon Peter travelled in Judea and Samaria (Acts 9-10) and visited Antioch according to Paul in Galatians 2:11. Later on, he evidently had strong ties with the churches in Bithynia and Pontus, Galatia and Cappadocia according to his letters (1 Peter 1:1-2).

JAMES, THE LEADER OF THE JERUSALEM CHURCH

Along with the Apostles and deacons one of the prominent leaders of the early community was James, the brother of Jesus. He played a major role in the emerging church and its teaching. He is specifically described as the brother of Jesus in Galatians 1:19 by Paul who meets him on his first visit to Jerusalem after becoming a Christian. Hegesippus, in the second century, refers to him as 'James the Just', others, 'James the Righteous', 'James of Jerusalem', and 'James Adelphotheos', the latter meaning James, the brother of God. In a letter addressed to this James from Clement of Rome, he was described as the "*bishop of bishops, who rules Jerusalem, the Holy Assembly of Hebrews, and all assemblies everywhere*" (Ernest Cushing Richardson and Bernhard Pick, eds. (1886), "The Ante-Nicene Fathers. C. Scribner's Sons, pp. 218-222).

We come across James in the Gospels. He is included a number of times generally and occasionally mentioned by name with the family of Jesus and with the brothers of Jesus (Luke 8:19-21). When people are discussing Jesus' identity and describing him as the carpenter's son, James is included in the list of his siblings. In John's Gospel, he makes the point that Jesus' siblings were almost cynical about his fame and Jesus' desire to keep his identity as the Messiah a secret. John's assessment of them was that they struggled to believe in him as the Messiah (John 7:3-5). There is no mention of the immediately family of Jesus being in Jerusalem for the last week of Jesus' ministry. Apart from Mary and her sister Salome, the family was notably absent from the cross or the resurrection appearances by Jesus.

A person called 'James' is mentioned in Paul's first letter to the Corinthians as one to whom Jesus appeared after his resurrection. This list of Paul's is the earliest mention of people who saw the risen Jesus, as Paul's letter was written before any of the other Gospels. It is interesting that Paul names only Peter and James among the many others who saw the risen Jesus (1 Cor. 15:3-8).

Most commentators identify this James with the James who emerges as the leader of the church in Jerusalem whom Paul identifies as the brother of Jesus. This would make this resurrection appearance to James as Jesus' brother a significant appearance. It would most certainly have been very important to James given his apparent indifference to Jesus before the resurrection.

The main sources for James' life after the resurrection are in Acts and Paul's letters. The Letter of James is traditionally attributed to him, and he is a principal author of the letter sent out after the Council of Jerusalem. Hegesippus in the fifth book of his Commentaries, says of James, *"After the apostles, James the brother of the Lord surnamed the Just was made head of the Church at Jerusalem."*

Jerome, in the fourth century, when translating the New Testament into Latin had a problem in describing James as the Lord's brother. The emergence of the doctrine of perpetual virginity of Mary did not allow that she had children after Jesus. So Jerome erroneously considered the term 'brother' of the Lord should be read 'cousin' and translated it accordingly.

We do not know at what point James became recognised as the leader of the church in Jerusalem. In the non-canonical writings of the second century such as the Gospel of Thomas, Jesus names James his successor: *"The disciples said to Jesus, 'We know that you will depart from* us. Who will be our leader?' Jesus said to them, 'Where you are, you are to go to James the Just, for whose sake heaven and earth came into existence" (Gospel of Thomas, Saying 12). Like much in these non-canonical gospels, these references cannot be received with much certainty, but reflect a widespread view held at the time.

In his letter to the Galatians, Paul recounts his visit to Jerusalem where he meets James for the first time. By this time James was already recognised with some seniority and having some sort of leadership (Galatians 1:18–19).

In Acts 15, we read the account of the first attempt to resolve the growing issue of the integration of Gentile converts into the newly emerging Christian communities. Many from the Jewish background were insisting that all new converts needed to adopt Jewish customs and practices, most importantly circumcision. This was causing considerable consternation not only in Jerusalem, but the confusion had spread to Antioch and also to the new churches in Galatia. In response to this, Paul and Barnabas visited Jerusalem to present the case from the Gentile perspective. It is here that Paul met James again. There was considerable discussion among the leaders about how to respond to the challenges of the new non-Jewish converts, if Paul's account in Galatians reflects an accurate assessment of the events. Paul says,

> "...they recognized that I had been entrusted with the task of preaching the gospel to the uncircumcised, just as Peter had been to the circumcised. For God, who was at work in Peter as an apostle to the circumcised, was also at work in me as an apostle to the Gentiles. James, Cephas and John, those esteemed as pillars, gave me and Barnabas the right hand of fellowship when they

> *recognized the grace given to me. They agreed that we should go*
> *to the Gentiles, and they to the circumcised."*
> - *Galatians 2:7–9*

Luke's account of the events in Acts 15 gives James, the brother of Jesus a prominent role and makes him the mouthpiece of the gathered assembly.

> *"The whole assembly became silent as they listened to Barnabas*
> *and Paul telling about the signs and wonders God had done*
> *among the Gentiles through them. When they finished, James*
> *spoke up. "Brothers," he said, "listen to me. Simon has described*
> *to us how God first intervened to choose a people for his name*
> *from the Gentiles."*
> - *Acts 15:12–14*

He continued,

> *"It is my judgment, therefore, that we should not make it difficult*
> *for the Gentiles who are turning to God. Instead we should write to*
> *them, telling them to abstain from food polluted by idols, from sexual*
> *immorality, from the meat of strangled animals and from blood."*
> - *Acts 15:19–20*

James takes the leading role in the proceedings and it is his words that are described as being the judgment of the assembly. In many ways it follows the dictum "less is more". However, in the light of the subsequent challenge presented by the "judaisers" that Paul so vehemently opposes in his letter to the Galatians, this letter sent by the leaders in Jerusalem, seems very weak.

After Paul returned to Antioch, it was obvious that the issue was still not fully resolved. Peter had come to Antioch and was mixing with the Gentile believers until some people supposedly sent by James arrived.

> *"…before certain men came from James, he (Peter) used to eat with the Gentiles. But when they arrived, he began to draw back and separate himself from the Gentiles because he was afraid of those who belonged to the circumcision group. The other Jews joined him in his hypocrisy, so that by their hypocrisy even Barnabas was led astray. When I saw that they were not acting in line with the truth of the gospel, I said to Cephas in front of them all, "You are a Jew, yet you live like a Gentile and not like a Jew. How is it, then, that you force Gentiles to follow Jewish customs."*
>
> *- GALATIANS 2:12–14*

It is difficult to say how much of this behaviour was encouraged by James, but Paul took a very strong stand against it nonetheless. This was to be a major crisis for the early church and Paul's letter to the Galatians has this as its principle focus. Paul believes that this teaching by the Judaisers is another gospel and not the one received from Jesus. The theme of his letter describes very fully the reality that being 'In Christ' and being redeemed by him, results in us being placed in the position of sons and daughters to God the Father. Paul declares that it is for freedom that Christ has set us free. Galatians is most likely the first piece of Christian literature ever written.

Whether James, the brother of Jesus fully had this revelation we cannot know for sure. Yet there is a letter named after him in the New Testament but this has always been viewed with some concern since the earliest days of the church. Many of the early church Fathers, whilst knowing the work, did not consider it to be inspired in the same way as the rest of the New Testament. Martin Luther, in the sixteenth century, described it as an "epistle of straw." In reading through the epistle, its writer has a strong emphasis on obedience and good behaviour which are not in anyway wrong in themselves, but does not reflect the life and freedom that Paul is so eager to promote in Galatians and his other writings. I am left wondering if it exists as a testament to the early groups who were predominantly Jewish in background and who had some sort of allegiance to James and the style of Christianity he may have represented.

Paul's Response to the Challenge of the Judaisers
– the letter to the Galatians

The church faced a very significant challenge at this point. What was the gospel? Did it include circumcision and obedience to Jewish customs? Paul's response to the Judaiser challenge was to write a letter to the churches he had planted in Galatia. This was the first New Testament document written by Paul. Many scholars believe it was probably written about 47 A.D. from Antioch. It was written to churches in southern Galatia in the first century but was included in the Bible for the instruction of all Christians. Paul wrote the letter to disprove the claims of the Judaisers, who said Christians must follow the Jewish laws, including circumcision, to be saved.

Galatia was a province in the Roman Empire, in central Asia Minor. It included Christian churches that had been planted by Paul in the cities of Iconium, Lystra, and Derbe.

In this letter, Paul begins by defending his credentials as an apostle. He cites the Jerusalem apostles' acceptance of his gospel teaching and tells of his challenge to Peter to teach the true gospel (Galatians 1:1-2:14). In this first letter, he is very direct about the nature of the crisis and the impact of the Judaisers. He says they are teaching "another gospel".

> *"I am astonished that you are so quickly deserting the one who called you to live in the grace of Christ and are turning to a different gospel — which is really no gospel at all. Evidently some people are throwing you into confusion and are trying to pervert the gospel of Christ."*
> *- Galatians 1:6–7*

He says that the Galatians as a result are foolish and bewitched (Galatians 3:1).

The main theme of this letter is that keeping the law does not save us. Paul writes to counter the claims of these Jewish teachers that Christians need to obey the law in addition to their faith in Christ. Believers in Christ are justified by faith, not by works of the Law. Paul says that Abraham's belief in God was credited to him as righteousness. Paul makes it clear the Law serves to reveal our inability to obey. It is faith in Jesus Christ alone that saves us from our sins. Salvation is a gift from God the Father. We cannot earn righteousness through works or good behaviour. It is being in Christ that brings us into relationship with God and makes us sons and daughters.

> *"We who are Jews by birth and not sinful Gentiles know that a person is not justified by the works of the law, but by faith in Jesus Christ. So we, too, have put our faith in Christ Jesus that we may be justified by faith in Christ and not by the works of the law, because by the works of the law no one will be justified."*
> *- Galatians 2:15-16*

This letter is very significant in that it is a clear statement of the revelation that Paul had received directly from Jesus. It is what Paul was teaching and believed. It shows that for Paul, God the Father of the Lord Jesus was central to his thinking and that for Christians we are brought into a relationship with God as Father through our faith in Christ. He describes what it is like to live as sons and daughters and introduces the whole concept of sonship. All people who are baptized into Christ are one and are God's sons, Abraham's offspring and heirs to God's promise.

According to Paul, our sonship is a result of having been redeemed by the death of Christ. Through faith, we are then placed in a position of sons or as he says, we receive from the Holy Spirit, the Father's gift of sonship.

"But when the set time had fully come, God sent his Son, born of a woman, born under the law, to redeem those under the law, that we might receive the full rights of sons. Because you are his sons, God sent the Spirit of his Son into our hearts, the Spirit who calls out, "Abba, Father." So you are no longer a slave, but God's child; and since you are his child, God has made you also an heir" (Galatians 4:3-7).

In the final sections, Paul urges the Galatians to walk by the Spirit, bear each other's burdens, and do good to everyone. He gives a final warning to deny circumcision and follow the gospel of Christ. True freedom comes from the gospel, not from legalism. Jesus frees his followers from the bondage of Jewish law and tradition.

> *"For in Christ Jesus neither circumcision nor uncircumcision has any value. The only thing that counts is faith expressing itself through love."*
>
> - Galatians 5:6

The Spirit of God works in us to bring us to Christ and enables us to cry out to God as our Father. Salvation is not by our doing but by God's. God's love and peace flow through us because of the Holy Spirit. Further, the Holy Spirit enlightens, guides, and empowers us to live the Christian life.

> *"But the fruit of the Spirit is love, joy, peace, forbearance, kindness, goodness, faithfulness, gentleness and self-control. Against such things there is no law. Those who belong to Christ Jesus have crucified the flesh with its passions and desires. Since we live by the Spirit, let us keep in step with the Spirit"*
>
> *- GALATIANS 5:22–25*

In the conclusion of the letter, Paul writes,

> *"See what large letters I use as I write to you with my own hand!"*

Regarding this conclusion, Bishop Lightfoot, says in his commentary on Galatians:

"At this point the apostle takes the pen from his amanuensis and the concluding paragraph is written with his own hand. He writes a whole paragraph, summing up the main lessons of the epistle in terse, eager, disjointed sentences. He writes it, too, in large, bold characters that his hand-writing may reflect the energy and determination of his soul."

THE REVELATION OF SONSHIP – HUIOTHESIA

In Galatians, Paul introduces the revelation of sonship. He received this from direct revelation from Jesus. In Galatians 1 in defending his gospel he says,

"For I would have you know, brethren, that the gospel which was preached by me is not according to man. For I neither received it from man, nor was I taught it, but I received it through a revelation of Jesus Christ."

- GALATIANS 1:11-12

In the Acts of the Apostles, Luke records that when on trial before King Agrippa, Paul tells of his encounter on the Damascus road with the risen Christ.

"I was on the road. I saw a light from heaven, brighter than the sun, blazing around me and my companions. We all fell to the ground, and I heard a voice saying to me in Aramaic, "Saul, Saul, why do you persecute me? It is hard for you to kick against the goads." Then I asked, "Who are you, Lord?" "I am Jesus, whom you are persecuting," the Lord replied, "Now get up and stand on your feet. I have appeared to you to appoint you as a servant and as a witness of what you have seen and will see of me. I will rescue you from your own people and from the Gentiles. I am sending you to them to open their eyes and turn them from darkness to light, and from the power of Satan to God, so that they may receive forgiveness of sins and a place among those who are sanctified by faith in me.""

- ACTS 26:13–18

Paul speaks in this passage that Jesus tells him that he will testify of *'what you have seen and will see of me.'* In this, we have an indication of the revelations that Paul would receive directly from Jesus.

In Galatians, Paul introduces us to the term that I am translating as sonship. He uses a term five times in his letters that is difficult to translate. It is the Greek word 'huiothesia'. It appears first in Galatians 4:5. Then it is used in Romans 8:15 and 23, then again in Romans 9:4 and finally in Ephesians 1:5. This word is often translated to mean 'adoption' in English bibles and other Latin based translations such as French and Spanish. In the northern European language translations, the word is not rendered as adoption. In the New Testament itself, only Paul uses this word. Therefore, it seems reasonable to ask a very specific question, when Paul used this word, what did he mean by it? By his use of this word in Galatians 4, it seems that the English word 'adoption' does not fit the context, whereas "sonship" or something like it is precisely what Paul is talking about. The sons who have not yet come of age do not need to be adopted. But they do need to come into a situation in which they can exercise their full rights as sons. Paul makes clear his main concerns in the following two verses:

> *"As proof that you are sons, God sent the spirit of his Son into our hearts, crying out 'Abba, Father!' So you are no longer a slave, but God's child; and since you are his child, God has made you also an heir."*
>
> - GALATIANS 4:6-7

The translation of 'huiothesia' as adoption does not convey the meaning that Paul intends. The English word adoption refers to a legal process by which a person who wants can legally recognise and adopt a child who is not theirs biologically. Thus, the child will be officially recognised as their own, and consequently have the same legal status as any other children they may have. There are a number of reasons why adoption is not the proper English word to convey Paul's meaning in the passages where he uses *huiothesia*.

In English, adoption means that the child who is adopted is not your child in any sense before the adoption took place. This meaning conflicts with the way Paul uses *huiothesia* in Galatians 4:5.

Secondly, adoption in English refers primarily to the legal contract that makes a person one's child, whereas the meaning in Paul's use of *huiothesia* is as the end result of redemption. Redemption is the process by which God the Father reconciles us to himself and brings us into a position of sons in relationship with the Father.

Equally significant there is a serious emotional and psychological problem with using the word adoption. Many children who have been adopted are troubled about the fact that they are adopted. They may be very comfortable that their new parents wanted them and were happy to adopt them. However, they often wonder, who their birth parents were. Why did they not want to keep me? Many then try to seek out and locate their biological mother and father. In some cases, these kinds of thoughts can result in children suspecting that there must have been something wrong with them or that their birth parents did not want them and then gave them up. It is obvious that any thoughts of this kind are completely out of place in the contexts where Paul uses *huiothesia*.

In the situation Paul is referring to there are no other parents who have given up the children first so that God can adopt them. Indeed, in Acts 17:28 when addressing a Greek audience, he declares that we have always been God's offspring. God has always been our Father and we have always been his offspring, but we have lost the relationship because of the fall and our sin. He sends Jesus into the world to reveal that he is and always was Father and that through faith in Christ and his redeeming work on the cross, we are brought home and receive back our status as sons.

As Paul uses the term *huiothesia,* the meaning refers to the status of being a son. In particular to two facts that result from that status, first that we recognise ourselves to be God's child, and therefore we feel that it is right to address God as "Father." Paul connects this very strongly with the receiving of the Spirit of God in several passages (Romans 8:15-16; Galatians 4:6; Ephesians 1:13). Secondly, there is the fact that all of the promises that God has made to his people are made especially to us as his sons. As God's sons, we can expect to receive everything that God has promised to his people. Paul introduces the idea that we are God's "heirs" (Romans 8:17-25; Galatians 4:7; Ephesians 1:3-14).

It cannot be overstated that this first letter of Paul is of immense significance in setting out the doctrine of the revelation of God as a Father who redeems us and puts us in place as his sons. The doctrine of sonship is central to understanding the rest of the New Testament and God's dealings with mankind.

This teaching by Paul in Galatians is foundational to all of Paul's other letters. In many ways, they are applications of this understanding of being 'In Christ' and therefore sons. Often, his other letters address specific pastoral situations and theological issues that have arisen in the churches he is connected with and with people he knows. He wrote the letter to the Romans at some point before he was taken as a prisoner to Rome and tells them that he very much looks forward to meeting them. Chapter 16 of Romans is an extraordinary list of people to whom he sends greetings which gives an incredible window into the people who were part of the early church. It was probably written from Corinth. In Romans, Paul expands and develops his teaching on the nature of the good news of salvation that Jesus has brought to us. It is a magnificent work, rich in Old Testament imagery and revelation of the truth that we are justified through faith of Christ and have peace with God as a result.

Paul's two letters to the Church in Corinth are windows into the life of the church in that city in the middle of the first century. As in all the introductions to his letters, he opens up the fact that God is the Father of our Lord Jesus Christ. In 2 Corinthians 1:4-6 he says,

> *"Praise be to the God and Father of our Lord Jesus Christ, the Father of compassion and the God of all comfort, who comforts us in all our troubles, so that we can comfort those in any trouble with the comfort we ourselves receive from God."*

In 2 Corinthians, Paul explains the way we have been reconciled to God by Jesus and that it was the initiative of the Father to reconcile us to himself.

The Prison Letters written probably from Rome: Ephesians, Philippians, Colossians, I and 2 Timothy, Titus and Philemon also carry this revelation of God as Father in his teaching.

There is evidence of another missionary journey by Paul after the end of Acts where he is last seen under house arrest in Rome. The evidence comes from Paul's own letters and was possibly around AD 62 - 68. According to Romans 15:24,28, Paul's intention was to visit Spain. Eusebius in the fourth century implies that Paul was released after his first Roman imprisonment. There are statements in early Christian literature that say he took the gospel to Spain. Also Paul mentions places visited in his letters not recorded in Acts.

It was believed that Paul was beheaded in Rome during a brief but violent outbreak of persecution in 67 AD. The church of San Paolo Fuori i Muri in Rome is supposedly built over his tomb.

Paul's revelation of God as the Father was profound. It permeates everything he writes. His classic description of being "in Christ" is his unique summary statement of the position that is ours as sons and daughters of God the Father. His use of language is very clear when talking about God. He differentiates which of the three persons of the Godhead he means. He often says 'God and the Lord Jesus Christ' using the word God almost as an abbreviation for God the Father. Other times, he amplifies this within the context to ensure that there is no doubt that when he means God, he means the Father. Ephesians 1:17 is a classic example.

> *"I keep asking that the God of our Lord Jesus Christ, the glorious Father, may give you the Spirit of wisdom and revelation, so that you may know him better."*

Each letter begins with a statement about the nature of God the Father and his relationship with his Son, the Lord Jesus Christ and also with the Holy Spirit.

Paul is thoroughly Trinitarian albeit using the Greek language and not Latin. The Latin word Trinity as a description of the threefold nature of the Godhead came later, as we shall see. For Paul, the whole nature of the Godhead was about a loving relationship that they want to share with all humanity.

In summary, it can be said that the Apostle Paul is the great exponent of our status in Christ and therefore as sons of God. Sonship is possible because of who God is as our Father and what Jesus has done for us on the cross. And the Holy Spirit pours the love of God as a Father into our hearts (Romans 5:5).

Paul says he received these revelations directly from Jesus. He says in Galatians,

"I received it by revelation from Jesus Christ.

...when God, who set me apart from my mother's womb and called me by his grace, was pleased to reveal his Son in me so that I might preach him among the Gentiles, my immediate response was not to consult any human being."
- Galatians 1:12, 15- 16

The judaiser crisis was the catalyst that resulted in a very clear statement of foundational Christian thought and belief. It came as revelation directly from the Father through Jesus, just as the revelation of God being our Father was revealed through the life and ministry of Jesus.

Whilst Galatians may be the first piece of Christian literature ever written, it builds on a foundation of the experiences of people who had met Jesus. These eyewitnesses faithfully reported what they had seen and heard Jesus say and do. Much later, in the first century, the Apostle John in the introduction to his letter says,

"That which was from the beginning, which we have heard, which we have seen with our eyes, which we have looked at and our hands have touched —this we proclaim concerning the Word of life. The life appeared; we have seen it and testify to it, and

we proclaim to you the eternal life, which was with the Father and has appeared to us. We proclaim to you what we have seen and heard, so that you also may have fellowship with us. And our fellowship is with the Father and with his Son, Jesus Christ."

- I JOHN 1:1-2

Peter writing in his second letter says of this testimony,

"For we did not follow cleverly devised stories when we told you about the coming of our Lord Jesus Christ in power, but we were eyewitnesses of his majesty. He received honor and glory from God the Father when the voice came to him from the Majestic Glory, saying, "This is my Son, whom I love; with him I am well pleased." We ourselves heard this voice that came from heaven when we were with him on the sacred mountain"

- 2 PETER 1:16-18

Beyond any doubt, the writers of the New Testament were mostly eyewitness of the events they describe or were very closely associated with those who had met and known Jesus personally, heard him speak or had been part of the very earliest Christian community. The Apostle Paul towers above all of the other New Testament writers both in quantity and depth of revelation, closely followed by the Apostle John. In the next chapter, we look at the reason why they wrote and the truth that they write about.

The Gospels and the Revelation of God the Father

Early in the first century, as eyewitnesses to the events surrounding the life and ministry of Jesus began to die, there was a growing need to write down what they had experienced. In reading through the Gospels, we cannot ignore the authentic detailed content of many of the stories. They have such a ring of truth and eyewitness quality about them. There are a growing number of Christian writers and theologians who are revisiting these documents through the eye of not only faith but also critical analysis. Richard Bauckham, in his book *Jesus and the Eyewitnesses* says that Mark was the earliest and "that the other three canonical Gospels - Matthew, Luke and John, were written in the period when living eyewitnesses were becoming scarce, exactly at the point in time when their testimony would perish with them were it not put in writing."

Bauckham explores the whole nature of this eyewitness testimony that is found in the Gospels. He says, "An irreducible feature of testimony as a form of human utterance is that it asks to be trusted. Trusting testimony is not an irrational act of faith that leaves critical rationality aside; it is, on the contrary, the rationally appropriate way of responding to authentic testimony. The Gospels understood as testimony are the entirely appropriate means of access to the historical reality of Jesus."

He continues, "Theologically speaking, the category of testimony enables us to read the gospels as precisely the kind of text we need in order to recognise the disclosure of God in the history of Jesus. Testimony enables us to read the Gospels in a properly historical way and a properly theological way, it is where history and theology meet" (Bauckham, *Jesus and the Eyewitnesses,* Eerdmans Publishing Co. 2006).

In the Gospels, we have the narrative accounts of the life and ministry of Jesus. On a casual reading, we can see that the first three gospels are very similar and that the last, John's Gospel is quite different. Yet together, they create a picture of the unique nature and person of Jesus and his relationship with God his Father and how he reveals the Father.

The first three gospels: Matthew, Mark and Luke.

The Gospels of Matthew, Mark and Luke share so much in common that they are called the 'Synoptic' Gospels meaning that they frequently cover the same events in similar and sometimes identical language. It is believed they were written around the middle of the first century. Most scholars and commentators agree that Mark's Gospel was probably the earliest written and was used like a template by Matthew and Luke or at least as a major source for them. Much of Mark's Gospel is included word for word in their versions of the life of Jesus.

Many other scholars see another major source that Matthew and Luke both used in their Gospels. This source consists mainly of sayings or teachings of Jesus. Scholars refer to them as 'Q'. There may have been an early document that recorded some of the sayings that was circulating among the early church.

In looking at the individual writers and the style of their Gospels, it helps us see what their reason for writing was and how they handle the revelation of the Father that Jesus brings.

If we begin with Mark's Gospel, what do we know about it? We know quite a lot about John Mark, the person traditionally identified as the writer of the gospel. He first appears in Acts 12. It is to his mother Mary's home that Peter goes after he is released from prison by an angel. The church had been gathering there to pray for his release. This places John Mark as a resident of Jerusalem in the early period of the days of the church. Also, it potentially places him in Jerusalem in the final week of Jesus' life. It is quite possible that in that last week, Mark may have encountered Jesus and witnessed many of the events that he later records in his Gospel from Chapter 11 to the end. Many think that it was his mother's house that Jesus used for the last supper.

It was thought that John Mark was also the same person described as a cousin to Barnabas, the traveling companion of Paul, based on Colossians 4:10. At the end of Acts 12, Saul, that is Paul and Barnabas who had been in Jerusalem returned to Antioch *taking with them John, also called Mark.*

In Acts 13, when Saul and Barnabas set off on the first missionary journey they take John Mark with them and he stays with them while on Cyprus. However, when crossing over the mainland again they came to *"Pamphylia, where John left them to return to Jerusalem"* (Acts 13:13).

Luke later says that Paul and Barnabas parted company over the issue of Mark's early departure, Acts 15:36-39.

We do not know what John Mark did after that, though Peter mentions him in his first letter (1 Peter 5:13), where he refers to him as "my son Mark". This is generally accepted to be the same Mark as mentioned in Acts. At some point, Mark and Paul are reconciled as Paul mentions him in his second letter to Timothy.

> *"Get Mark and bring him with you, because he is helpful to me in my ministry."*
>
> — 2 Timothy 4:11

Apparently Mark was with Paul during his first imprisonment in Rome when Paul wrote the four prison epistles: Ephesians, Colossians, Philemon, and Philippians. Paul mentioned the same Mark in Philemon 24, which was written at the same time and carried by the same letter carrier, Tychicus, to the receivers in the city of Colosse.

From a very early date, the Church accredited the second of the four Gospels to Mark. According to Papias of Hierapolis, writing in the early second century, this Gospel was by *"Mark, (who) having become the interpreter of Peter, wrote down accurately, though not in order, whatsoever he remembered of the things said or done by Christ."* Other early writers such as Irenaeus of Lyon in Gaul (about 177 AD) agreed with this. *"No early church tradition and no church father ascribes the Gospel to anyone other than Mark."*

On reading through Mark's Gospel, it can be noted that Peter is often mentioned and not always in a very complimentary way. He is presented 'warts and all'. No attempt is made to sanitize Peter's failure. This is taken not as an attack on the character of Peter but more on his honesty in openness to his personal vulnerability, if indeed he was the primary source of much of Mark's writings.

It is Mark who, of all the gospel writers, records Jesus' prayer in the garden of Gethsemane where he addresses God as Abba Father.

The Gospel of Mark does not appear to have been written for a theological reason. If anything, it feels like it was written quickly. There is even doubt as to whether Mark ever finished the Gospel, as most of the earliest surviving copies seem to end suddenly at Mark 16:8. Some manuscripts from the third century onwards have endings added that are clearly not original. If the purpose was to simply record the reminiscences of Peter then this might explain the lack of theological intent.

Turning to Luke's Gospel, it is important to recognise that this gospel was the first volume of two works. The Gospel is by the same author as the Acts of the Apostles, which is the book that tells the story of the beginnings of the Christian church and focuses its last half on the life and ministry of Paul. It is very clear from the way the two books begin in the prologue to each one, that the same author wrote them and that the narrative continues from one to the next. So, the author of Luke and Acts is writing a two-volume work. The author is telling a bigger story, a grander story, a story that starts with Jesus and is concerned with his life and ministry. It then sees the story continuing with the beginning of the church and gospel is spread with the missionary journeys of Paul that eventually take him to Rome itself.

According to church tradition dating from the second century, the author was the Luke named as a companion of Paul in three of the letters attributed to Paul himself. He is a Greek and the only Gentile Christian writer of the New Testament. The language of Luke reveals that he is an educated man. We learn in Colossians 4:14 that he is the 'beloved physician'. In his two books, Luke refers many times to sicknesses and diagnoses. It is very possible that Luke provided medical assistance to Paul when he had been beaten, stoned or nearly drowned while evangelizing to the Roman Empire. Being a Greek and a doctor would explain his scientific and orderly approach to the book, giving great attention to detail in his accounts.

Material found in his Gospel and not elsewhere includes much of the account of Jesus' birth, infancy and boyhood. Also included are some of the most moving parables, such as that of the Good Samaritan and that of the Prodigal Son. Luke mentions three of the sayings of Christ on the Cross: *"Father, forgive them," "Today you will be with me in Paradise,"* and *"Father, into your hands I commend my spirit."*

Luke does not seem to have as strong an emphasis of God as Father as found in John's Gospel, rather he naturally weaves the references together as the story unfolds. He does so in such a way as to suggest an ease and familiarity in addressing God in this way. Note this example from Luke 12:32 where he records the words of Jesus to his disciples, *"Do not be afraid, little flock, for your Father has been pleased to give you the kingdom."*

It is Luke who gives the only incident in the years between Jesus' infancy and the commencement of his public ministry. It is very likely that Mary told him this along with the birth narratives. Significantly, it records Jesus calling the temple, "my Father's house" or perhaps that he was about his Father's business. Whatever the exact interpretation of Luke's Greek, the fact remains Luke is saying that as a young adolescent, Jesus knew and referred to God as his Father.

In Luke's account of the Gospel, we find an emphasis on the human love of Jesus, on his compassion for sinners and for suffering and unhappy persons, for outcasts such as the Samaritans, tax collectors, lepers, shepherds, and for the poor. The role of women in Jesus' ministry is more emphasised in Luke than in any of the other Gospels. He also unusually names a number of women who were part of the wider group of Jesus' followers. This was not typical of other writers in this age. Luke regularly gives people's names where in similar sections also found in Mark, that writer does not.

If he is using Mark's Gospel as a source, Luke both expanded on Mark and corrected his grammar and syntax. Mark wrote poor Greek compared to Luke and Paul. Some passages from Mark, Luke eliminated entirely, notably most of chapters 6 and 7. Despite this, he follows Mark's plot more faithfully than Matthew.

Despite being grouped with Matthew and Mark, Luke's Gospel has some parallels with John's Gospel. For example, Luke uses the terms "Jews" and "Israelites" in a way that is more characteristic of John than Mark. Notably, Mary, Martha and Lazarus are found only in Luke and John. At Jesus' arrest, only Luke and John state that the servant's *right* ear was cut off. Several such small details as these are found only in Luke and John.

Luke joins Paul's group of travelling companions in the book of Acts. Up until Acts chapter 16, the story is narrated in third person, much like an historian recording facts. Then the voice of the narrator changes to first person. Scholars believe this is done at the time Luke first joined Paul at Troas in the year 51. When the book of Acts switches back to the third person, many believe that this reflects a period of time when Luke was not present during the events that are recorded. One particularly significant time is while Paul is in prison in Caesarea for two years. It has been suggested that Luke used this time to travel around Galilee and Judea to collect much of his unique eyewitness material that he alone includes in his Gospel.

It is believed that Luke lived a long life and died about 74 AD in Greece. There are no stories suggesting he was martyred.

Turning to the first Gospel attributed to Matthew, it is difficult to say whether the Apostle Matthew is also the same Matthew who wrote the Gospel that bears his name. The Gospel itself does not say who wrote it, but the designation "according to Matthew" is very old.

Perhaps the Gospel was written by some early Christian, not an apostle, whose name was Matthew, and about whom nothing else is known. Early Christian readers, hearing the Gospel ascribed to "Matthew," would naturally associate it with the apostle of that name, and therefore the ascribing of the work to the Apostle Matthew becomes common at an early date, by a perfectly natural misunderstanding. Of course, it is equally possible that the Gospel writer is indeed the man named Matthew who was a tax collector and a disciple of Jesus. Matthew as a tax collector would have been used to recording lists and might have compiled this so called 'Q' document that contained the sayings of Jesus. We cannot be sure of this but it would seem likely. The argument can go either way.

Papias of Hierapolis, writing in the late first or early second century, says that Matthew compiled the sayings 'Logia' of Jesus in Hebrew. The material common to Matthew and Luke, but not to Mark, includes *will be found!* sayings of Jesus but almost no narrative. It has therefore been conjectured that there was once a document (usually called Q), now lost, that is *In Jesus' name* basically a collection of teachings by Jesus, and that Matthew, the Gospel writer and Luke had access to it while Mark did not. It has been suggested that Matthew the apostle is the author of this document Q, which may well have been first written in Hebrew or Aramaic. All this is highly speculative and circumstantial so there is not a lot of point in debating the issue.

What we have in the Gospel of Matthew is material that is common to Mark's Gospel and a large number of sayings that are unique to Matthew. There is also a strong emphasis on the fulfillment of Old Testament prophecy that is used to validate the legitimacy of the claims made by the early church to the Jewish community that Jesus was indeed the promised Messiah. Clearly, Matthew's Gospel was written for a Jewish readership. Some have suggested that it was written in Alexandria where there was a very large Jewish community.

In many of the sayings in Matthew's Gospel, there is a strong emphasis on the Father. References to the Father occur numerous times in the sayings and the Father is often described as 'my Father in heaven'. In Matthew 11:25–27, we read of a clear reference by Jesus to the revelation of the Father by the Son. The language is very akin to the language of John's Gospel.

> *"I praise you, Father, Lord of heaven and earth, because you have hidden these things from the wise and learned, and revealed them*

to little children. Yes, Father, for this is what you were pleased to do. All things have been committed to me by my Father. No one knows the Son except the Father, and no one knows the Father except the Son and those to whom the Son chooses to reveal him."

A common feature of all three gospels is seen in the above quote. Whenever Jesus addresses God personally, he always calls him Father.

THE GOSPEL OF JOHN

In turning to John's Gospel we find a document entirely different from the other three. This gospel more than any other book in the New Testament brings the fullest and richest revelation of the nature and heart of God the Father and how Jesus reveals him. John tells us that is what Jesus came to do.

"I have revealed you to those whom you gave me out of the world."
- JOHN 17:6

Nearly all bible scholars agree, *'the disciple whom Jesus loved'*, whilst he is not named in the fourth Gospel, is none other than John bar Zebedee. John the disciple and gospel writer was the son of Zebedee and the younger brother of James. According to the Gospels, their mother was Salome, a sister of Mary. James and John were therefore the cousins of Jesus. Zebedee and his sons were in business as fishermen in the Sea of Galilee. John had been a disciple of John the Baptist. Jesus then called these two sons of Zebedee to follow him. James and John did so and thus rank highly among the disciples of Jesus. They both held prominent positions for not only being the first of the disciples to be called, but also because of their relationship to Jesus. Jesus referred to the pair collectively as "Boanerges" which is translated "sons of thunder" in Mark 3:17. This name may have been given to them because although their nature may have been of a calm and gentle manner, when their patience was pushed to its limits their anger became wild, fierce and thunderous causing them to speak out like an untamed storm. At one point, John and his brother wanted to call down fire on a Samaritan town, but Jesus rebuked them (Luke 9:54–55).

At the last supper the *"disciple whom Jesus loved"* reclined on the couch to eat next to Jesus and leaned on to his chest. John, alone among the disciples, remained at the foot of the cross alongside Jesus' mother and his own mother Salome. As instructed by Jesus from the cross, John took Mary, who would have been his aunt, into his care. After Jesus returned to his Father and the outpouring of the Spirit, John, together with Peter, took a prominent part in the leading of the church. He is with Peter at the healing of the lame man in the Temple. With Peter, he is also thrown into prison. Again, John is with Peter visiting the newly converted in Samaria.

There is no information in the Bible concerning the length of time of this activity in Judea. According to tradition, John and the other apostles remained some twelve years, until the persecution of Herod Agrippa led to the death of his brother James and the scattering of the apostles throughout the Roman Empire and beyond. James became the first apostle to die a martyr's death according to Acts 12:2. John lived longer than James, by more than half a century.

Paul says he met John in Jerusalem, according to his letter to the Galatians. Paul, in his opposition of the Judaisers in Galatia, recalls that John explicitly, along with Peter and James the Lord's brother, was referred to as "pillars of the church". He says they recognised his apostolic preaching of a gospel free from Jewish law and released him to take the gospel to the gentile world.

Of the other New Testament writings, it is only from the three letters of John and the Book of Revelation that anything further might be learned of him. From this, we may suppose that John belonged to the multitude of personal eyewitnesses of the life and work of Jesus. Also, that he lived for a long time in Asia Minor and was thoroughly acquainted with the conditions existing in the various communities there. He held a position of authority recognized by all these churches as leader of this part of the church. Moreover, the Book of Revelation says that its author was on the Island of Patmos *'for the word of God and for the testimony of Jesus'*, when he received the visions contained in Revelation.

It is an issue of great debate among bible scholars when the Gospel of John was written. Some scholars agree in placing the Gospel somewhere between 65 AD and 70 AD. There is also a strongly held view amongst contemporary scholars that the Gospel was not written until the latter third of the first century AD, as late as 80 - 90AD.

Catholic tradition states that John went to Ephesus and from there wrote the three letters traditionally attributed to him. John was allegedly banished by the Roman authorities to Patmos. According to Tertullian in *The Prescription of Heretics*, John was banished after being plunged into boiling oil in Rome and suffering nothing from it. This event would have occurred during the reign of Domitian in the late first century. While he was exiled on Patmos in the Aegean Sea, he received the visions that we refer to in the New Testament as Revelation.

When John was very old, he trained Polycarp who later became Bishop of the church in Smyrna. Polycarp taught Irenaeus and passed on to him stories about John. In one of Irenaeus' works against various heresies, he relates how Polycarp told a story about John and the Gnostic teacher Cerinthus.

> *"John, the disciple of the Lord, going to bathe at Ephesus, and perceiving Cerinthus within, rushed out of the bath house without bathing, exclaiming, "Let us fly, lest even the bath-house fall down, because Cerinthus the enemy of the truth, is within."*
>
> *- Irenaeus, Adversus Heresies*

It is traditionally believed that John lived to an extreme old age, dying naturally at Ephesus in about AD 100. An alternative account of John's death, ascribed by later Christian writers to the early second century bishop Papias, claims that he was slain by the Jews. John's traditional tomb is thought to be located at Selcuk, a small town near Ephesus.

John's writings reveal God as Father
through the life and teaching of Jesus

In looking at John's works, he has a revelation of Jesus as the Son of God and how he reveals the Father perhaps more than any other. His Gospel is so much more than an historical account of Jesus' life. It is also a reflection of all aspects of the life of Jesus inspired by the Holy Spirit. It is John in his Gospel who record's Jesus telling his disciples,

> *"I have much more to say to you, more than you can now bear. But when he, the Spirit of truth, comes, he will guide you into all the truth. He will not speak on his own; he will speak only what he hears, and he will tell you what is yet to come. He will glorify me*

*because it is from me that he will receive what he will make known
to you. All that belongs to the Father is mine. That is why I said
the Spirit will receive from me what he will make known to you."*

- JOHN 16:12–15

At the end of his Gospel, he says,

*"Jesus performed many other signs in the presence of his disciples,
which are not recorded in this book. But these are written that
you may believe that Jesus is the Messiah, the Son of God, and
that by believing you may have life in his name."*

- JOHN 20:30–31

John's understanding of the central core of the Christian message is
so clear. Jesus continually reveals the Father. In the great prayer in John
17, John records Jesus' final words in the upper room. He says that Jesus
has completed his mission,

*"I have brought you glory on earth by finishing the work you
gave me to do."*

This extraordinary declaration by Jesus is said before his death on the
cross. He then says in 17:6 that he has revealed the Father to them. The
reality of this statement means that the cross is to be seen through the
revelation of God as a Father whose love for the world leads to his desire
to be reconciled rather than a judgemental God demanding retribution
and satisfaction for sin. Later, theologians beginning with Tertullian
seem to have missed this point.

John's letters written also towards the end of his life reflect a similar depth of revelation. In his letters, he calls for us to love one another, for love comes from God. To John, God is love. God the Father showed his love among us by sending his one and only Son into the world that we might live through him.

John also has a deep understanding that our relationship with God as a Father brings us into a position of sonship. He does not use the same language as Paul, John refers to the children of God rather than sons but the intention and meaning is the same. Like Paul, he says we are "in him" (1 John 1:5) and the evidence of that is walking as Jesus walked in fellowship with the Father as sons. He describes our sonship and position in Christ as making us the children of God.

"See what great love the Father has lavished on us, that we should be called children of God! And that is what we are."

- 1 JOHN 3:1

This is love to John. It is not that we loved God, but that he loved us and sent his Son as an atoning sacrifice for our sins. John has a rich Trinitarian understanding. He says we know that we are in him because he has given us of his Spirit.

John's last words according to church tradition were, "*So little children, let us love one another.*"

Of the other New Testament writers, there is a letter by James the brother of Jesus already referred to. Also another brother of Jesus, Jude wrote a short letter and then Peter and the unnamed writer of the letter to the Hebrews. All these writers refer to God as father, Jesus as the Son and the Holy Spirit as also divine. They are intuitively Trinitarian.

CHAPTER THREE

The Post-Apostolic Era

We do not know very much about the other apostles or the how their lives ended except from the traditions of the Early Church that may not be very reliable. More is recorded of some than others. Whilst Andrew and Thomas did not write any of the documents of the New Testament, there is quite a large amount of tradition associated with them from the early centuries.

ANDREW, THOMAS AND PETER

Андрей

The fourth century Church Father, Eusebius, in his church history quotes Origen's writing in the early third century, as saying Andrew preached in Scythia, Asia Minor and along the Black Sea as far as the River Volga in modern day Russia. According to other traditions, Andrew founded the church of Byzantium (Constantinople) in AD 38, installing Stachys as leader or bishop. Stachys was Bishop of Byzantium from AD 38 to AD 54. He seemed to be closely connected to Andrew and Paul. This church would later develop into the patriarchal church of Constantinople having the Apostle Andrew as its patron saint. It was not clear if Stachys was the same person as the one Paul calls "dear" in his letter to the Romans (Rom. 16:9).

According to Hippolytus of Rome (235 AD), Andrew preached in Thrace and his presence in Byzantium is also mentioned in the apocryphal Acts of Andrew written in the second century.

Andrew was said to have been martyred by crucifixion in the city of Patras in western Greece. Early texts, such as the Acts of Andrew known to Gregory of Tours (594 AD), described Andrew as bound, not nailed, to a Latin cross of the kind on which Jesus had been crucified.

Thomas is included in the list in the upper room in Acts and was there for the outpouring of the Spirit on the day of Pentecost. Eusebius of Caesarea (320 AD) quotes Origen as having stated that Thomas was the apostle to the Parthians but Thomas is better known as the missionary to India through the Acts of Thomas which was perhaps written as late as about 200 AD.

Thomas is believed to have left northwest India when invasion threatened and traveled by vessel to the Malabar Coast possibly visiting southeast Arabia and Socotra en route. He then landed at the former flourishing port of Muziris in about 51–52 AD in the company of a Jewish merchant. From there, he is said to have preached the gospel throughout the Malabar Coast. The various churches he founded were located mainly on the Periyar River, its tributaries and along the coast where there were Jewish colonies. He reputedly preached to all classes of people and had about 17,000 converts, including members of the four principal castes. Although little is known of the immediate growth of the church, Bar-Daisan (154–223) reports that in his time there were Christian tribes in India who claimed to have been converted by Thomas and to have books and relics to prove it. But at least by the year of the establishment of the Second Persian Empire (226), there were bishops of the Church of the East in northwest India with laymen and clergy alike engaging in missionary activity.

According to tradition, Thomas was killed in 72 AD.

Peter is listed first among the twelve disciples in the gospels and in the Acts of the Apostles (Acts 1:13). He is also frequently mentioned in the Gospels as forming with James and John a special group within the Twelve. Peter is often depicted in the Gospels as spokesman of all the disciples. Luke, the author of Acts, portrays Peter as an extremely important figure within the early Christian community, with Peter delivering a significant sermon on the day of Pentecost. According to Acts, Peter took the lead in selecting a replacement for Judas. He was twice arraigned, with John, before the Sanhedrin and directly defied them. He undertook a missionary journey to Lydda, Joppa and Caesarea, becoming instrumental in the decision to evangelise the Gentiles having preached to and baptising the Roman centurion Cornelius and his household (Acts 10).

About halfway through, the Acts of the Apostles turns its attention away from Peter and to the activities of Paul. The Bible is mostly silent on what occurred to Peter after this.

Acts 12 tells how Peter was put into prison by King Herod but was then released by an angel. At the Council of Jerusalem in about 50 AD, Paul and the leaders of the Jerusalem church met and decided to embrace Gentile converts. Acts portrays Peter as successfully opposing the Christian Pharisees who insisted on circumcision of the Gentile Christians.

Peter, also called Cephas, is mentioned briefly in Paul's letter to the Galatians, which describes a trip, by Paul to Jerusalem where he meets Peter (Galatians 1:18), and a trip by Peter to Antioch where Paul rebuked him for treating Gentile converts as inferior to Jewish Christians. These are the earliest references to Peter since Galatians is the first piece of written Christian literature.

Church tradition ascribes the letters, First and Second Peter to the Apostle Peter, as does the text of Second Peter itself.

Papias (130 AD) reported that the Gospel of Mark was based on Peter's memoirs, a tradition accepted by most scholars today. *"Mark,"* says Papias, according to the testimony of Eusebius (*Ecclesiastical History,* 3. 39), *"becoming the interpreter of Peter, wrote accurately, though not in order, whatever he remembered of what was either said or done by Christ; for he was neither a hearer of the Lord nor a follower of Him, but afterwards, as I said, [he was a follower] of Peter, who arranged the discourses for use, but not according to the order in which they were uttered by the Lord."*

To the same effect, Irenaeus (*Against Heresies,* 3,1) wrote, *"Matthew published a Gospel while Peter and Paul were preaching and founding the Church at Rome; and after their departure (or decease), Mark, the disciple and interpreter of Peter, he also gave forth to us in writing the things which were preached by Peter."* And Clement of Alexandria is still more specific, in a passage preserved to us by Eusebius (*Ecclesiastical History,* 6. 14), *"Peter having publicly preached the word at Rome, and spoken forth the Gospel by the Spirit, many of those present exhorted Mark, as having long been a follower of his, and remembering what he had said, to write what had been spoken; and that having prepared the Gospel, he delivered it to those who had asked him for it; which, when Peter came to the knowledge of, he neither decidedly forbade nor encouraged him."*

Eusebius continues, *"The apostle, when he knew by the revelation of the Spirit what had been done, was delighted with the zeal of those men, and sanctioned the reading of the writing (that is, of this Gospel of Mark) in the churches"* (Ecclesiastical History, 2. 15). In another of his works, Eusebius writes a similar statement, *"Peter, from excess of humility, did not think himself qualified to write the Gospel; but Mark, his acquaintance and pupil, is said to have recorded his relations of the actings of Jesus. And Peter testifies these things of himself; for all things that are recorded by Mark are said to be memoirs of Peter's discourses."*

In a strong tradition of the Early Church, Peter is said to have founded the church in Rome with Paul, and served as its bishop and then met martyrdom in Rome along with Paul.

In the epilogue of the Gospel of John, Jesus hints at the death by which Peter would glorify God, *"when you are old you will stretch out your hands, and another will dress you and take you where you do not want to go."* Some interpret this as a reference to Peter's crucifixion. Tertullian mentions the death of Peter at the end of the second century, and Origen is quoted in *Eusebius,* Church History III.1, *"Peter was crucified at Rome with his head downwards, as he himself had desired to suffer."*

Early church tradition also says Peter probably died by crucifixion with arms outstretched at the time of the great fire of Rome in the year 64 AD. According to the apocryphal Acts of Peter, he was crucified head down. Tradition also locates his burial place where the Basilica of St. Peter was later built, in the Vatican, directly beneath the Basilica's high altar.

Clement of Rome in his *Letter to the Corinthians* (Chapter 5), written between 80 – 98 AD, speaks of Peter's martyrdom in the following terms, *"Let us take the noble examples of our own generation. Through jealousy and envy the greatest and most just pillars of the Church were persecuted, and came even unto death… Peter, through unjust envy, endured not one or two but many labours, and at last, having delivered his testimony, departed unto the place of glory due to him."*

In Peter's sermons recorded in the Acts of the Apostles, it is primarily the fact of the resurrection of Jesus that Peter focuses on. It was necessary in a Jewish context to emphasize this in order to proclaim Jesus as the Messiah, the Christ and by implication the Son of God. To the Jews this would have been shocking as the concept of God having a son was as challenging as him being a Father. In Peter's two letters, it is possible to see that he had a revelation of God as Father, as well as a clear understanding of the nature of Jesus as the Son of God. Like Paul, he begins his letters by addressing praise to God the Father.

The Acts of the Apostles indicates something of the hostility of the Jews and secular authorities to the emerging church, and Peter warned in 1 Peter 4:12, *"Dear friends, do not be surprised at the painful trial you are suffering, as though something strange were happening to you."* This animosity seems to have become even more intense after the time of the apostles.

EARLY PERSECUTIONS

In Revelation 2:12–13, the reference to Pergamum being the place 'where Satan has his throne' is taken to mean the temple built for the worship of the Roman emperor, Augustus, and as the Roman Empire increased its dominance, so the Roman emperors increasingly demanded personal worship from all their subjects.

Beginning with Augustus, most emperors were declared to be divine and temples and shrines were built to venerate and worship them all over the empire. This was generally seen to have a unifying influence, but caused a huge conflict for Christians. The Christians were the natural enemies of this idolatry, and centuries of persecution by successive emperors developed.

Following the close of Acts, there were localised persecutions initiated by the Emperor Nero in 64 AD. Nero made Christians the scapegoats for the great fire of Rome and had many arrested and executed with great cruelty. He was able to select these particular victims with the support of his own people, as Christianity had been much maligned by rumours and false accusations. It was commonly believed that Christians were atheists because they denied all other gods and religions. It was widely believed that they were cannibals because they ate the body and drank the blood of their founder. Another widely held view was that they were incestuous, because they loved one another and addressed each other as brothers and sisters. Finally, they were considered killjoys who would never take part in pagan festivals, feasts and orgies.

The Jews were jealous for their traditions and there was a growing hatred expressed by the Jews towards Christians. There is a lot of evidence that shows the Jews were often the instigators of some of the localized persecutions. They also appeared to be jealous of the success of the Christian preachers.

The people of the Roman Empire, out of ignorance, hated Christians.

The Roman historian Tacitus describes them as *"a class hated for their abominations"*. But they were also pitied. Nero's barbaric cruelty *"gave rise to a feeling of pity...for it was felt that they were being destroyed not for the public good but to gratify the cruelty of an individual"* (Tacitus). There is no clear evidence that this persecution spread beyond Rome. News of Nero's action would have reached the provinces and provincial governors might have felt they could take similar action. The martyrdom of Peter and Paul belongs to this period. There were no persecutions recorded during the reigns of Vespasian (69 - 79) and Titus (79 - 81).

As a result of this sort of reputation, after the time of Nero, Christians became the natural targets to blame for any type of disaster. Tertullian, a leader of the church in North Africa in 200 AD, remarked, *"If the Tiber reaches the walls, if the Nile does not rise to the fields, if the sky doesn't move or the earth does, if there is a famine, if there is a plague, the cry is at once: "The Christians to the lion!" What, all of them to one lion?"*

The fall of Jerusalem in 70 AD marked the end of the Jewish state and the church in the city fled before its siege to Pella in the Trans Jordan area.

During the reign of Domitian (81 - 96) there was further outbreak of persecution though the evidence is somewhat ambiguous. The Emperor's cousin Flavius Clemens and the consul Acilius Glabrio were put to death, and Flavia Domitilla the emperor's daughter was banished to the island of Pontia. They were all accused of 'atheism' as this was a common charge against Christians and Jews for not having gods. Suetonius says Glabrio was condemned as a revolutionary. Eusebius believed them to be Christians (H.E. III, 17 - 20, New Eusebius p.8ff). There may have been sporadic persecutions but there was nothing in general. 1 Clement was written about this time (96 AD) from Rome and speaks about *"the*

sudden and repeated misfortunes and calamities which have befallen us."
This suggests a pattern of persecution on a local scale was commonplace
for the church.

However, the first century saw the rapid spread of the Gospel
throughout the Roman world mainly in the larger cities particularly in
the east but also in major centres such as Rome and Carthage and Lyon
in Gaul in the west.

THE SECOND GENERATION OF LEADERS
– THE APOSTOLIC FATHERS

The major preoccupation of the early Christians was to organise the
church to be a guide and support to its members as they sought to live
out their faith in a hostile world. There was not time or opportunity for
great thinkers to emerge. The church was a home in which Christians were
encouraged and equipped. Changing patterns of leadership developed
as the first generation of leaders died. Churches were encouraged to
"appoint bishops and deacons". This is the modern translation of the Greek
words 'episcopos' (bishops) and 'diaconos' (deacons). The ongoing need
for teaching and a desire to communicate and keep in touch resulted
in a second generation of writers and teachers emerging who were not
as clear and inspired as the first century writers had been. Also, what
we have is fragmentary. It is interesting to read their writings to get the
flavour of their language, terminology and interest. Second generation
writers did not have a complete collection of the New Testament as yet.
Some churches had more complete lists and others included some of the
writings of this second generation as part of the "scriptures". What they
all had was the Old Testament. So when they talk about God, it is very
much through the eyes of an Old Testament view of God and how the

predictions of the Old Testament where fulfilled through Jesus.

One of the first of these second generation writers was Clement of Rome who wrote a number of letters in the last quarter of the first century. He was the leader or 'bishop' of the church in Rome. He wrote two letters to the church in Corinth in which he refers to Paul's letters and sought to clarify issues of leadership. He writes about elders whom he describes as presbuteroi and or episcopoi and deacons. He also appeals to the Corinthians to end their schism and be united. His writings reveal that there is already a shift away from the revelation found in the New Testament.

Clement blends Old Testament themes with Greek ideas and expressions. He quotes extensively from the Septuagint and also quotes the words of Jesus, some of which are not found in the canonical gospels. There is a strong tendency to moralise and define what he considers Christian behaviour as imitating the Creator's good works. His crowning argument is not the victory of Christ over sin and death but the mythological tale of the Phoenix.

Clement is already viewing life from a legalistic perception or as James Jordan has described it, "eating from the wrong tree" that is the tree of the knowledge of good and evil that was in the Garden of Eden.

> *"For this reason righteousness and peace are far from you, since each has abandoned the fear of God and grown defective of sight in his faith, and ceased to walk by the rules of his precepts or to behave in a way worthy of Christ. Rather does each follow the lusts of his evil heart, by reviving that wicked and unholy rivalry, by which, indeed, "death came into the world"*
>
> - LETTER TO THE CORINTHIANS CAP II.

Here is one of few quotes where he specifically mentions God as a Father that can be found in his writings:

> *"The all merciful and benevolent Father has bowels of compassions towards those that fear him and kindly and lovingly bestows his favours upon those who come to him with a simple mind"*
>
> - SECOND LETTER TO THE CORINTHIANS CAP.XXIII

This is typical of the second generation of Christian writers. They are known as the Apostolic Fathers. There are not many of them and only some of their works have survived. We know there were more from the snippets of quotations that are found in the writings of later Christian writers.

Another was Ignatius of Antioch who was 'Bishop' of the church in Antioch in Syria. He was recognised as having a prophetic gifting. He had been a disciple of the Apostle John in his early days. In his writings, the leading presbuteros is referred to as episcopos, i.e. bishop in a church. He attacked the heresy of Docetism that said that Christ only appears to be human. There were already those in the churches who were saying that Jesus was not fully human. Docetists believed that human flesh, that is the body, was sinful and that Jesus would have been tainted by sin if he had a human body. Ignatius also wrote about martyrdom that was a growing experience for many in the Christian community and a major cost to be counted in becoming a Christian. He wrote about this while he was on his way in chains to Rome where he was martyred in 117 AD. He wrote seven letters on this journey. He speaks frequently of "the Father" throughout his epistles and brings the Father into closest connection with the spiritual life of a Christian. But he is not clear how that happens except as an extension of our relationship with Christ.

There does not seem to be the heart connection that the New Testament describes as sonship.

This is also true in the writings of Polycarp of Smyrna. One of his letters addressed to the Philippians survives. He was born in 70 AD and knew John the Apostle. He would have been about 30 years old when John died. Polycarp died a martyr in 156 AD. His letter is full of New Testament quotes; containing more references than any other work of the period. He is perhaps best known for his martyrdom. When asked to denounce his faith in Jesus Christ, he is recorded as replying,

> *"86 years have I served him and He has done me no wrong, how can I then blaspheme my King who saved me?"*

One of the most intriguing writers from this early period was Papias, Bishop of Hierapolis. Born in about 60 - 70 AD, he had heard John the Apostle and was a friend of Polycarp. He gathered the unrecorded sayings of the first generation of Christians. Only a few tantalising fragments remain, such as his comment, *"Mark recorded the reminiscences of Peter"*. He had millenarian ideas believing in the imminent return of Jesus. As a result, Papias was not well reported by later writers like Eusebius, a fourth century writer who said of him, *"(Papias) evidently was a man of very poor capacity as one may say judging from his own statements."* It is a pity that Eusebius did not like him, he might have told us much more if he had. By the fourth century, Millenarianism had fallen into discredit and with none more than Eusebius.

There is a letter from this time called *The Epistle of Barnabas* but this is not by the Barnabas "son of consolation" of Acts. It is more likely an Alexandrian work from about 130-140. In his work there is a passing reference to the Father. He is denouncing the empty ritualism of the Jews and says,

> *"We ought, therefore, being possessed of understanding, to perceive that gracious intention of our Father; for he speaks to us, desirous that we, not going astray like them, should ask how we may approach him."*
>
> *- EPISTLE OF BARNABAS*, CAP.II.

A work called *The Shepherd of Hermas* produced around 140 - 150 AD was extremely popular but not very good. Many churches included it in their list of approved 'Scripture'. It was an allegory written by a Roman Christian with no disciplined theological thinking and mostly concerned with post-baptismal sin. It failed to understand grace as the forgiveness of sins extending continuously through the whole of life. There is a diminished emphasis on the Person of Christ with an emphasis on striving for moral living and for conformity to the law. It taught that martyrs were saved by their sufferings: *"if you had not suffered for the Name of the Lord you would have died because of your sins"* and *"the sins of all these have been taken away because they suffered for the Name..."* The writer of the *Shepherd of Hermas* was a preacher of repentance rarely quoting from Scripture directly but using scriptural imagery and occasional phrases. This type of writing is typical of a trend to move from relational living as sons of the Father to going back to living from the legalism typified by eating from the wrong tree.

Perhaps the most important and widely read book from this period is *The Didache* also know as the *'Teaching of the Twelve Apostles.'* However, it clearly was not authored by any one of the twelve apostles. It was a handbook of church discipline and hardly mentions the great Christian truths that are centralities. Instead it deals with baptism, communion, fasting and how to recognise a true apostle or prophet. Some of its directives seem very bizarre to the modern mind. We are discouraged from fasting on Mondays and Wednesdays as the hypocrites do. Instead, real Christians fast on Tuesdays and Fridays! The way it was so widely circulated and used for centuries in the early church deemed its importance. It was seriously considered to be "scripture" by many, but its content was all about regulations and control of practice in the church.

These early works began to circulate widely and throw light on the changing face of the church and the growing impact of legalism and Greek philosophy on the church. The church was becoming increasingly less charismatic and more formal and organisational. The post apostolic era had lost the centrality of sonship that was defined by relationship and was increasingly replacing this with a system of rules and regulations. The sense of revelation and anointing is sadly absent from the few writings that remain from this time. It is hard to know how ordinary Christian believers would have lived and how they would have practiced their faith other than to have followed the instructions in these writings of the so called Apostolic Fathers.

CHAPTER FOUR

Opposition and Expansion

The Christian message spread over the next decades and there was great expansion in the east especially in Egypt in the region around Alexandria, which became a major Christian centre. Many fragments and copies of the scriptures have been found in the desert sands of Egypt. A recent discovery of a face mask that was placed on a mummified body from the late first century was found to be made up of sheets of papyrus. Scientists have been able to read these fragments and found some to be part of a very early copy of Mark's Gospel. This may be the earliest fragment of any of the New Testament dating from around 70 – 80 AD.

PERSECUTION INTENSIFIES

Asia Minor and Gaul had large Christian communities, as did other major cities but increased localised opposition grew. During the emperor Trajan's reign (98 - 117), Symeon the bishop of Jerusalem was martyred in 107 AD, and as aforementioned, Ignatius was martyred 117 AD.

There was an exchange of letters between Pliny the Roman governor of Pontus-Bithynia and the Emperor Trajan in 112 AD that are of immense importance because they deal with the issue of the persecution of Christians. Trajan says that Christians are not to be sought out and anonymous accusations are never to be used in criminal charges. If Christians were brought to court and convicted and then they recanted, demonstrated by sacrificing to "our gods", then a full pardon was to be given. Pliny's letter gives illuminating insight into Christian worship and how widespread the church was in that area in the second century.

The Emperor Hadrian (117 - 138) in his letter to Minucius Fundanus sent about 125 AD would not permit enemies of Christians to *"use mere clamorous demands"*, instead accusations were to conform to accepted legal procedure and anonymous accusers would be given heavier penalties.

In 156 AD, there was persecution of the church in Smyrna during the reign of Antoninus Pius (138 - 161). A Christian leader and apologist, Justin Martyr, writing during this reign says, *"You do not examine charges but...punish without investigation or consideration."* Christians were now suffering through mob violence and instigation of their enemies, especially the Jews. The Jews at Smyrna took prominent part in the persecution of Christians by collecting fuel for fire on which the old Bishop Polycarp was to be burned. *"The Jews as usual showed themselves specially zealous in the work,"* (Martyrdom of Polycarp, XII, 2, XIII).

During the reign of Marcus Aurelius (161 - 180) there was widespread persecution. In Rome (165 AD), the trial and death of Justin Martyr took place. Justin was born in Samaria in about 100 AD, converted in 130 AD and by 150 AD had established a theological school in Rome. He wrote several apologetic works including one to the Jews called 'A Dialogue with Trypho". He wrote to the emperor and also to prominent senators. In his *Second Apology* speaking of the *"Father of all"*, he says, *"These words, Father and God, Creator and Lord, and Master, are not names but are titles derived from his good deeds and functions" (Second Apology* cap.vi.). Justin gives a very clear picture of church life in the second century. In 165 AD, the authorities raided the school and many of its students were tortured and executed including its founder.

What is beginning to emerge in the writings of these apologists is a tendency to write about the universal Fatherhood of God rather than the relationship of the Father to his sons and daughters that the New Testament describes as sonship. The influence of Greek philosophy is beginning to be felt in this in which it talked about God as being a universal creator and father.

In Gaul, around 177 AD, there were horrific attacks on the church in Lyons and Vienne. Forty-eight people were martyred including the Bishop Pothinus who was aged 90 and a slave girl named Blandina whose courageous death deeply impressed the onlookers. One of the presbyters, Irenaeus, survived to record the events. Even worse, in North Africa, 180 were martyred in Scilli. The martyrs in North Africa from that time began to be "remembered" by the church there. The anniversaries of their deaths were celebrated and the graves visited. Stories of their heroic deaths began to circulate to encourage others who were facing such trials. This understandable human reaction sadly led the church down a path towards a form of teaching about martyrdom, the 'saints', relics and veneration of the dead that is far removed from the original intention. Martyrdom began to be seen of itself as akin to salvation.

THE SPREAD OF THE GOSPEL ACCELERATES

While many Christians died for their faith, the church grew in size and reputation. Christians were particularly noted for their lifestyle and works of charity. '*How these Christians love one another*', said one observer, and their love extended to the poor, widows, orphans, prisoners and slaves. Husbands were known to love their wives and to be faithful to them, in contrast to many of the pagans. Money for the church was expected to be used first to feed the poor, rather than on ornate buildings or rich vestments.

As one example, a record shows that the church in Rome at the year 251 AD supported one bishop, forty six presbyters, seven deacons, seven sub deacons, forty two acolytes, fifty two exorcists, along with readers and doorkeepers, together with as many as 1,500 widows and others in need.

The church continuing the work of preaching the gospel, spread very rapidly in Syria, Asia Minor and Greece. When the apostle Paul arrived as a prisoner in Rome, he found a large church already, and this spread to other Italian cities. Tertullian and Origen writing in about 210 AD referred to expansion even to the '*barbarous island of Britain*', and three British bishops attended the Council of Arles in 314 AD. A fourth century Roman villa discovered at Lullingstone in Kent was found to include a large Christian chapel, supporting the view that by the time of the Roman departure from Britain in 410, Britain contained a significant number of Christians.

The gospel flooded through North Africa to the extent that Tertullian was able to assert to the pagan Roman world, "*You are but of yesterday and we have filled all you have - cities, islands, forts, towns, assembly halls, even military camps, tribes, town councils, the palace, senate and forum. We have left you nothing but the temples.*" The Christians themselves were amazed at the speed and extent of church expansion before Constantine. It is hardly surprising that the church felt itself to be riding on the crest of a wave and faced the world with that confidence which was a marked feature of the early apologists.

THE PROLIFERATION OF UNBIBLICAL TEACHING

Since its very beginning in the book of Acts, we have seen that the early church was plagued by false doctrine and teachers who wanted to preach their own version of what they perceived the gospel to be. They were to trouble the church for centuries to come, right up to the present day with their unbiblical teaching.

Early in the first century, teaching began to circulate that is difficult to define but was a mixture of Christian truth, pagan myths and Greek philosophy. Today, this is generally called Gnosticism.

These people who are referred to as Gnostics were a large collection of unconnected and odd groups. Similar to the so called "mystery religions" of the East and not dissimilar to various aspects of new age teaching of today, the word Gnostic comes from the Greek word 'gnosis' meaning knowledge. However, it is hard to define Gnosticism because it is a vague term covering a vast range of ideas. It has come to refer to the pursuit of higher, superior knowledge. Basically, it was an early form of super spirituality, which claimed to have insight or revelation beyond that of 'ordinary' Christians.

The challenge for the church was that it threatened to transform Christianity into an Eastern mystery religion. About a dozen Gnostic sects, each with their own secret and superior knowledge, broke from the church between 80 and 130 AD, mostly hating each other as much as the church. Essentially, they distinguished between soul and body, the

75

former good and the latter evil. This implied ascetic living and ignoring the body for one group, and indulging the body in any way for another. They advocated the Greek idea of immortality of the soul rather than resurrection of the body, and denied that Christ could have taken on a human body. They were essentially seekers after hidden truth who had acquired special insight given to an elite few. So Gnosticism is a modern term applied to these various groups that challenged and embarrassed the church seriously in the first two centuries.

Christian leaders responded to these new cult-like groups in a variety of ways. Writing against these new groups became the major focus of Christian thinking for most of the second century and it gives insight into the development of Christian theology and teaching. In many ways, it was reactionary and quick to state what was right and what was not. The response of the Church was significant in the way it gave great importance to the scriptures and to the establishment of an approved "ministry" or leadership and also very significantly for the purposes of this book, the creedal formulas that were beginning to emerge. Christian writers who sought to explain Christian teaching and to expose the error of the various Gnostic teachers are know as Apologists.

A brief description of two of these groups helps understand the reaction by the Apologists and why certain aspects of Christian truth and thinking were so important and discussed.

One of the largest Gnostic groups, the Marcionites were known to trouble the church for centuries. The founder after whom the group is named was Marcion. He was a born in 85 AD, the son of the bishop of Sinope in Pontus, so he grew up in a Christian family. His main teaching included the rejection of the Jewish elements of the scriptures preferring the writings of Luke and Paul. He taught that the God of the Old Testament was bad and that the God of the New Testament was the Father of Jesus and was a God of Love. His followers were very strict and ascetic, rejecting sex and marriage. They drew up a list of New Testament books that they felt were inspired, rejecting books such as Matthew, Hebrews and James particularly because of their Jewish flavour. By the mid second century, Marcionism was by far a greater threat to the church than other forms of Gnosticism because it was more Biblical and plausible. Marcion was very literal in his interpretation of the Old Testament. For example, in the fall recorded in Genesis 3, God asks Adam, "Where are you?" Marcion deducted from this that the god of the Old Testament had limited power because he did not know where Adam was. It was this inadequate god that persuaded the Jews to kill Jesus. The danger of such teaching is that a focus on a sentimental view of God as a loving Father replaced a more robust biblical understanding of God as a Father. It was also a reaction to the continuing battle in early Christianity to retain Jewish practices within Christianity.

In the second century, the Montanists emerged. They were followers of Montanus. He led a group who wanted to return to the simple Spirit-led life of the book of Acts but also got into extreme discipline and super spirituality. They rejected the increasing rigidity of church worship and its lack of spontaneity. They were intensely interested in eschatology and believed that the Parousia, that is the second coming, would happen if there were enough expressions of kingdom reality on earth. They resisted the low moral standards of the world and promoted self-denial of the flesh and virginity. They also opposed the intellectualism of the church preferring the ecstatic utterance of their prophets. There was great emphasis on dramatic personal experience. We only know about them from those who opposed them so we may not have a fair understanding of what they believed.

Two women were recognised as prophetesses by the group, Priscilla and Maximilla, who had visions and prophesied and assisted Montanus. Montanism was very successful in Asia Minor and Gaul. One of their greatest converts was Tertullian who became a Montanist late in life, more of him later. It is debatable whether they were heretical or even Gnostic in the light of the modern Charismatic movement, though there were extremes, which were reported by their enemies.

The movement was both popular and widespread. As one would expect the response to its challenge was varied in different parts of the Christian world. Charges of moral laxity were made against the Montanists. Members were accused over finances and their preachers and prophets living in luxury. This may or may not have been true and is reminiscent of modern accusations leveled at similar characters in the Pentecostal world of North America. Prophetic claims were examined and discussed widely by the church. Tertullian commented on the result of this that the church *"Drove out prophecy…and put to flight the Holy Ghost."* He recognised that in a desire to define doctrine and protect the church from error and extremism it had actually devalued genuine prophecy and lost the spontaneous leading of the Holy Spirit.

The church actively opposed all these heretical groups including the Montanists. As a result of this, the church virtually abandoned the doctrine of the Second Coming at this time. In an attempt to deal with these issues the leaders of the church, the clergy, became hierarchical and controlling. They began to be the only ones who could administer communion and officiate at baptisms. Impassioned preaching was discredited and charismatic gifting viewed with great concern and skepticism.

WHICH BOOKS ARE TRUE?

Throughout the second and third centuries the growing church grappled with the issues of numerical increase and a spread of teaching that was not considered the true gospel. There were numerous books and letters circulating that some churches accepted and others did not. The Gnostics had additional Gospels and Epistles of their own, but it raised the question, which - if any- of these books were "inspired"? Paul's letters had been collected late in the first century and were widely used by the majority of the churches. Matthew, Mark and Luke were brought together by 150 AD. Irenaeus writing in Lyon in Gaul stressed that the real test was whether the books were by the apostles, or by men closely connected with them. Irenaeus called those that were apostolic, 'Scriptures'. A little later, Tertullian in North Africa was referring to the New Testament, which he placed on a level with the Old, as being of divine inspiration.

By 250 AD, Origen writing in Alexandria in Egypt was accepting most of the New Testament, though Hebrews, James, 2 Peter, Jude and 2 and 3 John were disputed. The New Testament as we know it was finally agreed upon by the Council of Carthage in 400 AD. This became known as The Canon of Scripture.

WHICH DOCTRINES ARE TRUE?

The second major development was about theology. What was Christian truth and what was not? The process of defining Christian truth continued over the next two centuries. Various bishops and theologians questioned and argued over doctrine. Most of the issues centred on the nature and person of Jesus as fully human and yet at the same time fully divine.

Various attempts had been made to define this but had fallen short in some way. Dynamic Monarchianism taught that divine power and wisdom came upon the man Jesus effectively limiting his divinity. Some thought that the divinity of Christ was a mere power bestowed on Jesus by God at his baptism. Therefore, he was only God for a limited period of time. Others believed there was no independent personality of Christ. They said that Father, Son and Spirit were different modes of the one God. This was referred to as Modalistic Monarchianism. As a consequence summaries of what Christians believed began to be circulated and discussed. These eventually became standardised as Creeds.

Early creeds were essentially a series of questions addressed to new converts at their baptism, their answers having been taught to them in the process of teaching and preparation leading up to their baptism. These new converts were known as catechumen and their instruction was referred to as the catechism.

WHO SAYS IT IS TRUE?

This raised the question of who said what was true and what was not? Who were the true teachers? Who could teach the catechism in any church?

It began to be taught that only those churches and bishops that could trace their spiritual heritage back to the Apostles were true churches. Lists were made of the succession of bishops in the larger churches. This became known as Apostolic Succession and was used to attack the heretical origins of some teachers. Independent teachers became less common by the end of the third century. Itinerant prophets and teachers had virtually ceased to exist in the church. The Didache had an interesting test on how to discern a true itinerant prophet. If they stayed two nights they were true prophets, three or more they were false. Also the real test was if they ordered food supposedly "in the spirit" and then ate it, they were definitely false. The church came to find its unity in the episcopate, which is the rule and authority of the bishop, and appealed to the supposed 'tradition', which had come down through the bishops. This subsequently led to the undue prominence given by the Roman Catholic Church to tradition that resulted in 'The Traditions of the Church' being placed along side the Scriptures as a basis for authority.

The challenge of the Montanists was to remain within the church for several centuries and was attacked by orthodox and heretical groups alike. The root of this was the question, what was Spirit led and what was not? *religion steps in* This led to the loss of the work and power of the Holy Spirit in most churches. There was no room for spontaneous prayer or participation by the ordinary people known as the laity. It became the norm for only bishops and presbyters who were being described as the clergy, to preside at all services especially baptism and the Eucharist.

In addressing these issues four great teachers emerged to face and respond to the challenges.

IRENAEUS – A SECOND CENTURY 'FATHERHEART' TEACHER
" French "

Irenaeus of Lyon (130 - 200 AD) was a native of Asia and had been a pupil of Polycarp in his early life in Smyrna. He spent time in Rome and later became a presbyter and bishop of the Church at Lyons in Gaul. When persecution of the Church at Lyons and Vienne broke out in 177 AD, he was away in Rome carrying a letter from the bishop of Lyon with a plea for toleration of the Montanists. In his writings, he describes

81

the sufferings of the martyrs in Gaul. With Irenaeus, we enter a new region of profound and detailed thought. He was the first constructive Christian theologian. His chief work, *Adversus Haereses,* is a detailed attack on Gnosticism. His rebuttal of the Gnostic teachings demanded a thorough and comprehensive treatment of all the biggest subjects of theology and the Christian life.

His arguments in refuting Gnostics were that heretics neither follow Scripture nor tradition. They ignore the succession of authorised teachers, which was the list of bishops. The church, he taught, was the guardian and repository of apostolic teaching. He said that heresies were of recent formation and they have no antiquity and nor did they go back to apostles. He said there was no mention of any other God in the Old Testament other than God the Father. Irenaeus said there were only four gospels. He said that the teaching of the church was uniform and universal. He emphasised Christ's reality and exclusiveness. Above all others, Irenaeus was the teacher who wrote about the Fatherhood of God in addressing these Gnostic heresies. He continually appeals to the Father revealed in the New Testament to answer these issues. He balances the righteousness and judgment of the Father with the mercy, grace and love of the Father.

How different the course of Christian theology in the coming centuries would have been if future theologians had Irenaeus' balance. He continually demonstrated that knowing God as Father involves living as sons in relationship with him through Christ his son. He sees this as a gift just to believers which he anchors in Romans 8:15. To Irenaeus, sonship comes by receiving the Spirit of Sonship from the Spirit as the Father's gift. However, he says that service to God as sons is expressed in obedience and in terms of God's sovereignty rather than relationship.

The subtle drift away from heart-based sonship begins to appear in many subsequent writers and theologians. With the growing loss of the spirit of sonship, the Fatherhood of God begins to lose its place in Christian theology.

A STEADY DRIFT AWAY FROM SONSHIP

The second great Greek-speaking theologian was Clement of Alexandria (150 - 215 AD). The need for instruction of young Christians had arisen and a leader called Pantaenus founded a school in Alexandria where Clement became his pupil. Clement was born about 150 AD in Athens to heathen parents. He converted to Christianity, travelled widely and was influenced by Greek philosophy, notably Platonism. He arrived in Alexandria about 180 AD and was a pupil of Pantaenus until 190 AD when he began leading the school. Clement stayed until about 203 AD when persecution broke out instigated by the emperor Septimius Severus.

Clement then went to Cappadocia. His writings emphasised evangelism, instruction for new Christians and practical Christian living. He answered the question, how does a Christian behave in a cultivated and sophisticated society? He said Christ is his tutor. For Clement, nothing was left to guesswork. Clement was writing for both educated and wealthy Christians. In all the greater towns at end of second century, Christianity had penetrated right into the upper classes. His was an attempt to establish a relationship between culture and Christianity, rather than the fanatical hatred of this world that was found in Tertullian.

For Clement, the teaching of salvation is all about *"the reconciliation of disobedient children to their Father"* (*Exhortation to the Greeks,* cap.i). He goes on to say, *"Abba Father, this is the true utterance of his children,*

God accepts with gracious welcome the first fruits he receives from them" (Ibid, cap. ix.).

His doctrine of salvation is significant. He says *"Being baptised we become sons; being made sons, we are made perfect, being made perfect we are made immortal"* (Pedagogue,i.6.). To Clement, baptism is the initiatory and grace-giving sacrament of the Christian life, but this is more in illumination rather than reconciliation with the Father. Clement had an emphasis on perfected knowledge that is given by the indwelling Word (logos) and the Wisdom of God. This tended towards showing salvation as coming by means of truth inwardly revealed by the Word rather than by means of the love of the Father awakening in us a loving response. This began to weaken the influence of God as Father who works through love and fills us with the awareness that we are his sons and daughters.

In the third century, the empire had a series of troubles including economic depression, army mutinies, frontier incursions by barbarian tribes, and revolts in some of the provinces that preoccupied the emperors. As a result, the third century saw a period of relief and advance for the church only checked by occasional outbreaks of persecution.

The person who took on Clement's thinking and role in Alexandria was Origen of Alexandria (185 - 254 AD). He had an excellent classical education in Alexandria. Origen was the son of Leonides who had been martyred. His own desire to follow his father in martyrdom was thwarted by his mother hiding all his clothes preventing him from running out into the street. After his father's death, Origen had to provide for the family so he settled down a little. He was a catechist at seventeen under Bishop Demetrius. Origen's approach to life was that of an ascetic with a great emphasis on purity and chastity. This led him to believe he should make himself a eunuch for the sake of the kingdom, which he did. He was widely travelled and visited Rome and other major Christian cities. He lectured to large numbers, and was frequently away from the catechetical school, making visits to various places and often consulted by leading people. He even had a correspondence with the Empress who wrote sympathetically to him. When the emperor Caracalla's troops sacked Alexandria, Origen left for Palestine and continued his ministry in Caesarea and Jerusalem. He founded a new school in Caesarea. During the persecution instigated by the emperor Decius, he was cruelly tortured before he was released as a physically broken man. He died in 254 or 255 AD.

As a theologian, his influence on Christian thinking has been very significant. He had an immense output of over 6,000 largely biblical books and letters. A team of stenographers paid for by a wealthy supporter assisted Origen. He had many good and kind friends. His literary activity continued over forty-five years.

The general consensus on Origen's theology is that where he is good, there is no one better. Where he is bad there is no one worse. He splendidly defended Christianity and wonderfully expounded scripture but his teaching on the divinity of Jesus left the door open in the next century to the heresy of Arianism. His work was full of references to the Fatherhood of God. He used his teaching about the Father to show that an eternal Father implies an equally eternal Son, who is timeless and changeless. This relationship in the Godhead never came into existence or will ever pass out of existence. However, he saw this relationship based in terms of wisdom rather than love. The Son of God is the Father's personal Reason, Wisdom and Word by whom he is made known and active throughout the universe. To Origen, our inclusion 'in Christ' enables us to enjoy the wisdom and rationality and moral qualities of God not as an entrance into Sonship however. For him, religion is explained with practically no reference to the fellowship of love with the Father.

J.S. Lidgett put it this way, "Though not absent from Origen's heart, love is absent everywhere from his theology except in its intellectual and moral elements. His doctrine of the Fatherhood of God, though present and supremely influential in all his writings, has lost all its gracious tenderness and much of its religious worth" (*The Fatherhood of God*, Bethany House 1987 p90).

TERTULLIAN – THE FIRST OF THE LATIN FATHERS AND THE SHIFT FROM HEART TO HEAD

At the turn of the third century, the first Christian theologian who was a Latin speaker rather than a Greek speaker began writing. This man was to begin the change that would realign the whole thrust of Christian theology until this present day. This is Tertullian of Carthage (155 – 240 AD). His writings included a strong defense of Christianity, which he addressed to the Roman authorities. He also vigorously attacked heresy and issued a call for strong discipline in church life and practical living.

Tertullian lived in Carthage in North Africa, modern day Tunis. His father was a centurion in the army. He had a pagan upbringing but was well educated. Very little is known of his early life but it is thought that he was probably a lawyer because of the huge amount of legal language he uses. He converted to Christianity around 195 AD in his forties. Tertullian would have witnessed the martyrdoms at Carthage in 180 AD when he was about 30. He made a massive literary contribution dating from about 197 AD and lasting about twenty years. Eventually, he 'converted' to Montanism. In his writings, he dismissed the charges of immorality that were continually aimed at Christians, stating they were good citizens and that only bad emperors persecuted them. He believed that Roman State and Christianity could co-exist.

Christian behaviour was an important theme for Tertullian. In *De Spectaculis*, he explains why believers do not attend games or the theatre, ending with the 'spectacle' of the Last Judgement. *De Oratione* is a superb study of the Lord's Prayer. *De Baptismo* attacked the novel practice of baptising infants, which was beginning to be practiced. In *De Poenitentia*, he discusses sin and repentance after baptism, allowing that there could be a second repentance. Later when he became a Montanist, he changed his mind and said there was no possibility of second repentance. Shortly after 200 AD, Montanism gained a foothold in North Africa and Tertullian became enthusiastic about their teaching. Their strict legalistic approach to life appealed to him and he began to look on the recognised church as lax and dead. He is one of the more colourful characters of early church history whose forthrightness and turns of phrase make for lively reading. Tertullian was the first to use the term 'Trinity'. *"...the mystery of the economy which distributes the unity into trinity, setting forth Father, Son and Spirit as three."*

He spoke of philosophy as a major cause of heresy. *"What has Athens to do with Jerusalem? What has the Academy to do with the Church? What have heretics to do with Christians?"* This was a sideswipe at the Greek theologians and church fathers who tried to accommodate Greek philosophy and merge aspects of it into Christian thought. He spoke famously of the so called heretic Praxeas, *"He did two good works for the Devil, he drove out prophecy and introduced heresy, he put to flight the*

Paraclete and put to death the Father." Tertullian, as a Montanist, saw his role in life to drive out heresy and introduce prophecy.

In Tertullian, we see the beginning of a shift away from the centre of Christian life and theology in the great cities of the east to the west, noticeably Rome. We enter a different cultural mindset and atmosphere. This had a tremendous impact on all aspects of Christian theology but most especially on the doctrine of God the Father. Latin brilliance began to mould Christianity and church thinking in the West in every way. Lidgett in his book on the *Fatherhood of God"* says "the practical, external temperament of the Romans, their tendency to hard legalistic moralism, and their narrow superstition became the tone of western Christianity for over a thousand years or more. Christianity was to become institutional, satisfied with religious ceremony and outward forms, morally self-satisfied and spiritually superstitious, expecting and submitting to ecclesiastical authority."

Like Tertullian, future teachers of Christian doctrine such as Cyprian of Carthage, Ambrose of Milan and, without a doubt, the greatest of them all Augustine of Hippo had been Roman lawyers and administrators before they became Christian teachers and clergy. Slowly over time, the teachers also became the church leaders and enforcers of western Christianity.

For Tertullian, it was natural to apply Roman understanding and legal terminology to his theology. He speaks very rarely of the Fatherhood of God. Rather, his language reflects the courtroom and the judgment hall. God is the Creator and Governor of the World. He is the Judge. In his importing of terms from Roman law for the first time, he uses the word 'satisfaction'. This is a Roman legal term that he used to describe God's requirement for man to repent of sin. After repentance, the wrath of God would be satisfied. The just demands of the Ruler and Judge that required satisfaction by the act of the penitent sinner are emphasized. However, this is at the expense of most of the grace and mercy of God the Father.

The Greek spoken in the east was the language used to formulate the Creeds. It was difficult for Latin speakers and readers in the west to grasp the subtleties of the phrases and terms used. The Creeds in time became enshrined into beliefs to be recited and laws and rules of conduct and Christian behaviour to be adhered to and obeyed. Church authorities enforced them in coming centuries with punishment inflicted on those who disobeyed or failed to believe them.

The west began to focus less on the Fatherhood and love of God and increasingly on the sovereignty of God that made religion a work of fear rather than a response of love to the Father. Mix this with deep superstition that was all pervading in Roman culture, add a fear of divine disapproval and the scene is set for the Dark Ages and Medieval Christianity, but that is jumping ahead. However, the seeds of all this are in Tertullian.

CHAPTER FIVE

The Development of Roman Christian Thinking

After a long period of peace and freedom from serious persecution during which the church grew and spread widely things suddenly changed. By the middle of the third century, the emperor Decius turned his attention toward the church. Decius' aim was a complete destruction of the church. The emperor wanted to be a religious and political reformer of a corrupt Empire. He thought a thorough return to ancient Roman worship would save the State. He saw Christianity as the Empire's most serious opponent. As a result, the persecution that he instigated was an official, universal and systematic persecution. It began on a fixed day everywhere in the Empire and left nothing at all to local initiative. Decius aimed more than anything else to destroy the church's prestige and to degrade Christians rather than make them martyrs.

SUDDEN AND WIDESPREAD PERSECUTIONS

1771 yrs in 2020

Its first phase, directed at Christian leaders, began in December 249. The bishops of Rome, Antioch and Jerusalem were all executed. The bishops of Carthage and Alexandria only escaped by going into hiding.

The second phase began in June 250 when he ordered a general sacrifice for the entire population. Those suspected of being Christians but who sacrificed had to obtain an appropriate certificate from the authorities, a 'libellus' to prove they had complied. Every effort was made to secure apostasy from Christians by the authorities.

Tragically, the success of the assault was immediate. The church was totally unprepared for this new wave of persecution. In Rome, Asia Minor, Carthage, Alexandria and other centres, Christians flocked in the thousands to sacrifice to the divinity of the emperor. Imprisonment and torture were severe threats and many weakened. The church had grown careless and weak. There were stories of heroism and fortitude and it would be wrong to underestimate them, but the general effect was humiliating.

Mercifully, the death of Decius brought the campaign to an abrupt end. There was a short period of peace at the beginning of the next emperor Valerian's reign. During this brief lull, many lapsed Christians returned to their churches seeking reentry into membership.

The return of the lapsed caused a huge problem and division in the church. A North African lawyer named Cyprian, who converted in 246 AD, became the bishop of Carthage in 248 AD just before the outbreak of persecution. During the troubles, he withdrew from the city reasoning that there would be less chance of accusations and attacks on the church if he were not there. Also, he felt he would serve the church better alive than as a martyr. On his return, he began to address the problem of the lapsed. Cyprian's solution was to insist on rebaptism of the lapsed. However, the bishop of Rome opposed this. Cyprian therefore called a council of bishops together in Carthage to discuss the issue.

The dominating theme for Cyprian was the unity of church. For him, everything made sense with this argument, *"He cannot have God for a Father who does not have the Church for a Mother"*. He also said, *"If any man was able to escape who was outside the ark of Noah, then will that man escape who is out of doors beyond the Church."* For Cyprian, his reasoning was that there was no salvation outside the church, and as a result baptism by heretical or schismatic groups was not valid.

Cyprian insisted that no one outside the true church could convey special grace for baptism or ordination. To Cyprian, heretical or schismatic baptism was outside the authentic church and without the sanction of a true bishop and was therefore lacking the Holy Spirit.

Cyprian's arguments were cut short as persecution began again in 257 AD. The new emperor Valerian's policy was an attempt to exterminate Christianity by attacking it as a society, its leadership and its meetings. The first edict in 257 AD forbade the assembly of Christians threatening death for bishops who refused to conform. Both Dionysius of Alexandria and Cyprian of Carthage were exiled under this edict. Cyprian was later beheaded.

The second edict in the summer of 258 AD codified punishment for Christians. In the new legislation, clergy were to be punished by death and senators and knights were punished through the loss of their rank and the confiscation of their property. If they persisted as Christians, they were to be killed. Ladies of rank were to lose their property and be exiled. Caesariani, that is, dependants of the Emperor were to be sent to work in chains on imperial estates. It was a time of turmoil throughout the empire. Once again, the death of the Emperor brought the persecution to an end as barbarian tribes invaded Italy and Spain. The Persians attacked Asia Minor and Valerian died, captured by the Persian army.

Forty years of peace and expansion followed giving relief to the church. During this time, the church of North Africa became dominated by a desire to venerate the martyrs. There was also controversy over forms of Christian worship. The doctrinal controversy continued over the readmission of the lapsed and whether they should be rebaptised. At the same time, there was growth in the organisation of the church all across the empire and church buildings started to be built everywhere.

However, persecution broke out again in 303 AD under the direction of Diocletian. At the end of the third century, Diocletian ruled the Empire. He shared his rule with three others under a theoretically foolproof system of succession. He divided the empire into four parts each ruled by a Caesar and he presided over the various parts. The first edict in February 303 AD ordered the burning of Scriptures, the destruction of churches and the banning of Christian meetings. Christians were deprived of all honours and dignities. Imperial freedmen were to be deprived of rank and made slaves. All were liable to torture and court proceedings.

The second edict in March 303 AD called for the arrest of the clergy. Diocletian's wife and daughter were compelled to sacrifice. The third edict in December 303 AD offered freedom to imprisoned Christians if they recanted. Torture was the penalty for refusal. This was intended as a relaxation of oppression but led to fearful atrocities. Many died under torture though sometimes governors tried to arrange the escape of Christians. The object of this third edict was to weaken Christian resistance by making as many apostates as possible but this largely failed.

In the fourth edict in April 304, penalties were now extended to laity as well. All Christians were commanded to sacrifice or be put to death. The effects, however, were spasmodic and localised. It was most severe in the East and did not strike everywhere with equal ferocity. In Gaul, Britain, and Spain, where the Caesar was Constantius, he was content to destroy a few churches and nobody was executed. In the eastern provinces and North Africa, persecution raged for nearly ten years owing to the malice of Galerius and his successor Maximian.

It is impossible to estimate numbers of those who suffered. Eusebius writing as eyewitness and sober historian in Caesarea tells of thousands who suffered in Egypt where as many as 30, 60 or 100 suffered in a single day. He wrote about multitudes of martyrs in Arabia, Asia Minor and Mesopotamia. When the persecution was finally over, the wreckage that remained within the church was appalling. The problems as a result were to influence the church in the East and West for some time to come.

In many ways, the church had been exceptionally successful over its first four centuries. Despite almost continuous persecution with thousands of men and women laying down their lives to proclaim Christ, the gospel had spread to most parts of the Roman world. Heresies of the most damaging kind had been encountered and refuted, important doctrinal issues resolved, and the New Testament recognised and accepted as the Word of God. The place of the clergy and the role of ministry, order and leadership had been established in the churches with care for the poor as a priority. This was probably the only institution in the ancient world with a conscience for the oppressed. On the other hand, there appears little mention of the Jews in this time period. Paul's prediction or prophecy in Acts 28:28, that *the gospel would now go to the Gentiles*, who unlike the Jews would listen, seems to have been the case in these centuries. Also, there was a reduction of the place given to the specific activity of the Holy Spirit, except among the Montanists, who despite the association with Tertullian, were marginalised and then excommunicated by the mainstream church. In the quest to 'batten down the hatches' against heresy, it is clear that little room was left for the spontaneous activity of the Holy Spirit through his gifts in the church. Nevertheless, it is impossible to see the general advance of the church in this period as anything but a mighty working of the Holy Spirit.

CONSTANTINE - THE FIRST 'CHRISTIAN' EMPEROR

Diocletian's plan to share the rule of the empire did not work and early in the fourth century, civil war erupted and the victor who emerged was Constantine who defeated his opponents at the battle of the Milvian Bridge, just outside Rome in 312 AD. Prior to the battle, Constantine had a vision in which he saw in the sky the sign of the cross and heard a voice say, *"In this sign conquer"*. He instructed his troops to paint the cross on their shields and they won the battle. This experience marks the beginning of his Christian phase and his conversion. One of the first actions that Constantine took was to publish an Edict of Toleration, which effectively gave official recognition to Christianity by the state.

The result of this toleration was official patronage for the church, particularly in the realms of tax and privilege. Constantine presented many gifts and offered special facilities to Christian clergy. In 312 AD, clergy became exempt from municipal office and statutory labour. There was a large increase in the numbers of Christians in responsible posts in the Empire. At this period, Constantine even forbade Christians or members of the upper classes from becoming clergy because he said their duty was to the State first. In 315 AD, lands belonging to clergy became exempt from tax. In 318 AD, facilities were granted for certain legal actions to be tried at bishop's courts, that is matters not normally dealt with other than in Roman law courts. Previously, only specifically Christian matters could be dealt with at bishop's courts. In 321, bequests to the church were legalised, especially land. Sunday was declared a public holiday, as "the venerable day of the Sun". Many imposing church buildings were erected during Constantine's reign. The first church dedicated to St. Peter was built on Vatican hill. The Church of the Holy Sepulcher was built at the emperor's expense in Jerusalem between 327-335 AD. The emperor's mother Helena, a former bar maid from York, was keenly interested in seeking out sites of sacred significance for churches and became an avid collector of holy relics. She apparently found a large piece of the 'true cross' that she brought back to Rome and had a church built to house it that became know as Santa Croce. She was a fourth century Indiana Jones.

The effect of imperial favour was not wholly healthy, however. The hope of pleasing the emperor and the desire of sharing in the privileges he granted to Christians induced many posing to be Christians to seek admission to the church. Constantine's favour popularised Christianity and it became commonplace to regard a citizen as automatically Christian. Walter Hilton says, "So many fish were brought into Peter's net that it was well nigh to breaking." It brought unworthy elements into the church and the ease with which Christianity could be practised lowered the standards. Historian Dean Inge went so far as to say, "After Constantine there is not much that is not humiliating."

The new era of respectability, following being given the status of official religion of the Roman Empire, was a mixed blessing for the church. After Constantine, much would depend on the quality and attitudes of the emperors who succeeded him, and their relationships with the church, largely under the leadership of the Bishop of Rome.

The transition for the church from persecution to respectability had obvious disadvantages, but there were benefits as well. Many more people than otherwise were brought under the influence of the Christian ethos, and had the opportunity to hear the gospel. The Christian faith powerfully affected legislation with respect to the value of human life, the rights of all people, including slaves and barbarians as well as citizens. Adultery was punished, concubinage forbidden, divorce made difficult, and the status of women improved. Crucifixion as a means of execution was banned and the exposure of unwanted babies on rubbish dumps forbidden. The Christian faith and its application in society had beneficial effects on general morality.

On the other hand, the new attitude to Christianity had the adverse effects of making Christians intolerant to opposition and choosing to use physical power rather than truth to settle arguments. The increasing lack of distinction between Christian and worldly activities led to an escalation of pagan practices coming into the church such as images, veneration of the saints, and particularly non-Christian perceptions of Mary. The hierarchical nature of the church became overemphasized with bishops becoming supreme, taking on secular authority, and dominating rather than caring for their flocks. The church itself became a secular, persecuting power and the distinction between church and state became fuzzy.

Through the efforts of Constantine, the church became a unified organisation. In fact, just at the time when the Roman Empire was poised to diminish in its authority, the church was increasing in its authority, an authority that was taking on an increasingly secular nature.

ARIANISM – AN ATTACK ON THE NATURE OF JESUS

Following Constantine's conversion, controversy developed over the nature of Jesus and the church began a period of great internal turmoil and division. It is tragic that no sooner had the persecutions ceased, the church turned upon itself and a great struggle began over doctrine. However hard this was, there was truth at stake and the church needed to hold on to that truth and define it in order to save Christianity from sinking into error and deception.

Arius a leader from Alexandria began to dispute the divinity of Christ in 318 AD. He taught that only God the Father was eternal and too pure and infinite to appear on earth. Therefore God produced Christ the Son out of nothing as the first and greatest creation. It was the Son who then created the universe. God then adopted the Son. As a result, this made his nature inferior to that of the Father and thus robbed him of his divinity. Also, Arius taught that the Holy Spirit was the first and greatest creation of the Son. Bishop Alexander of Alexandria took issue with Arius reaffirming that Christians have always worshipped Jesus as God. He said he was "co-substantial and co-eternal with the Father".

The seriousness of this challenge to orthodoxy became apparent to Athanasius (296-373 AD), a deacon in the church in Alexandria and he became the champion of orthodoxy in the struggle against this new heresy. He was to emerge as the chief opponent of Arianism and had one of the most brilliant minds that the church had produced to date. His grasp of biblical truth and the significance of the dangers presented by Arius was second to none. The church owes him a great debt of gratitude. He wrote an outstanding work called *On the Incarnation* which defines the doctrine of Christ's divinity and humanity. Five times, he was exiled when Arianism gained the upper hand in Alexandria. Each time, he went to Ethiopia where he evangelised and planted churches.

The nature of the disagreement is complex and turns on just one letter, the Greek letter i – iota. Arius claimed that Jesus was of similar essence – 'homoiousios' - with the Father. Athanasius argued that Jesus was of the same essence – 'homoousios' - with the Father. There is a great deal of difference between similar and same! The controversy raged for years with whole churches adopting Arius' views. It was said, *"The whole world was split over an iota."*

ATHANASIUS – A CHAMPION OF TRUTH AND SONSHIP

This was no ordinary controversy. It hit at the very heart of the gospel and the nature of salvation by attacking the divinity of Jesus and made him lesser than the eternal Son of God. Athanasius, in his book, undertook a thorough scriptural examination of how the New Testament describes the relational and eternal nature of the Father and the Son. The focus of his work is on the impact of this relationship on Sonship for those who are in Christ. He resists the trend to view God's Fatherhood as universal to all mankind but defines it magnificently to those who are redeemed by the Son. God is Father to all those who through Christ, his only begotten Son, have received the spirit of Sonship. It is the incarnation of the Son that brings this, according to Athanasius.

Athanasius places greater stress than any other previous teachers on the sonship of Christians, stating that we become sons as the climax of the incarnation. He shows how the Son's divinity enables him to impart the spirit of sonship into the hearts of those who enter into relationship with him. It is the gift of the eternal Father to humanity through his Son.

C. Baxter Kruger in his assessment of Athanasius says of him, *"For Athanasius, it is unthinkable that God would turn his back upon His creation. The work of God in creation flows out of the endless love of the Father, Son and Spirit. If God were suddenly to turn cold towards the human race, such a turn would indicate that coldness, indifference or neutrality is part of the relationship of the Triune God – or else that God is suddenly acting contrary to the way the Father, Son and Spirit have existed from all eternity"* (*Jesus and the Undoing of Adam*, Perichoresis, 2007).

Athanasius stands alone as perhaps the greatest and clearest exponent of the nature of the Son in his relationship with the Father and to humanity as sons of God. He is also perhaps one of the last to fully grasp this point as the focus increasingly shifts to the west and Roman thinking.

Constantine called a great gathering of church leaders together which became known as the Council of Nicaea in 325 AD to attempt to resolve the issue. The council ruled in favour of Athanasius regarding his position as scriptural. Arius was banished, but his views spread nonetheless. The reality was that most did not understand the point at issue so they were vague in explaining the outcome to their churches. This lack of theological clarity over the next decades meant that the battle against Arianism was almost lost with whole provinces and churches succumbing and becoming Arian.

There were troubles in North Africa following the great persecutions. The church was split between those who supported a harsh and strict approach to those who had lapsed during the great persecutions. This included many who venerated the martyrs and those who wanted a more conciliatory approach. Mensurius, the bishop of Carthage managed to keep the sides together until his death in 311 AD. On his death, two candidates for bishop were put up representing the two different factions.

The rigorists included powerful landowners and over 70 local bishops. One of the most outspoken rigorists was Lucilla the Bone-Kisser. She was a passionate collector of martyrs' relics and bones and proposed one of her servants, Majorinus as the new bishop of Carthage. She had a personal dislike for the other candidate Caecilian who was ultimately elected. The result was two bishops. When Majorinus died in 313 AD, Donatus became the champion of the rigorist faction. This resulted in a break away church led by Donatus as the bishop of Carthage.

Both sides appealed to the emperor who appointed Miltiades, the bishop of Rome to arbitrate. Constantine the Emperor ruled in favour of Caecilian and condemned Donatus. This was ratified at the Council of Arles in 314 AD. Donatus then complained that the Emperor had interfered in church matters. Many churches in North Africa became Donatists and there was opposition to the Catholics, as the western churches were being called, and also to the imperial officers in the province. Constantine responded by confiscating Donatist property.

Donatism took on a nationalistic and fanatical flavour with groups arming themselves and attacking imperial armies with the hope of being martyred in the fray. The dispute went on for most of the century and only began to decline in the fifth century. Throughout the dispute, the Donatists saw themselves as the true church of the martyrs and the rest as soft on sin and repentance.

CHAPTER SIX

Theology Defined
and the End of the Empire

In order to bring unity and resolve doctrinal issues, the church gathered together bishops and theologians into councils. This became a major feature of the church in the next two centuries. The theory was that these councils would be representative of the whole church and would resolve the difficulties. In most cases, the Emperor was instrumental in bringing these about because of his concern for disunity within the church and, as a result, within the empire. Christian doctrine as we know it was defined at these councils by theologians and doctors of the church, but rarely did they resolve difficulties and disputes. If anything, they created more.

THE GREAT COUNCILS OF THE CHURCH

The first council held in Arles in southern Gaul (France) in 314 AD saw bishops come from as far away as Britain. Many who attended bore the scars of persecution on their bodies. It sought to resolve the schisms that had emerged over the lapsed in Egypt and the Donatist controversy in Carthage. This did not succeed as Donatism continued for more than another hundred years.

In 325 AD, at the great council in Nicaea, which is in modern day Turkey, Constantine himself presided. The council's aim was to refute Arius and define clearly the nature of Christ. They did manage to produce the Nicene Creed as a summary of doctrine. 318 bishops from Spain to Persia attended. Other issues agreed upon were the date of Easter, and the decision not to allow bishops to move sees - that is from one church to another and the recognition of the senior bishops in Rome, Alexandria, and Antioch in the church. Whilst the council had produced a creed, its implementation failed hopelessly with years of trouble and an alarming spread of Arianism.

At Constantinople in 381 AD, the Emperor Theodosius I called a council in an attempt to bring unity to the warring factions within the church. This was between the Arians and everyone else. There were schisms in Antioch and Constantinople over Arianism with rival bishops being appointed. The main theological achievement was to confirm the divinity of the Holy Spirit and make an unambiguous Trinitarian confession. The place of the bishop of Constantinople was recognised as being senior bishop after the bishop of Rome. This was not accepted by Alexandria that claimed priority in the East. At this time, Rome was seen as the most senior church of them all. What was clear was that rival cities and their bishops were vying for power and status in the wider church.

At Ephesus in 431 AD, a council tried to resolve a dispute between Nestorius the bishop of Constantinople and Cyril the bishop of Alexandria. Nestorius opposed the growing move to venerate Mary and to describe her as the Mother of God, the Greek word for this was, 'theotokos' meaning God bearer. Cyril, supported by many monks from Egypt, saw this as a blow to the heart of the church and demanded Nestorius' expulsion.

Rome sided with Alexandria and Antioch with Constantinople. There were dreadful scenes at the council with bishops and their bodyguards brawling and fighting. Nestorius was condemned but when John of Antioch arrived late to the Council, he announced the decision null and void and declared Cyril a heretic. There were fights and lots of very undignified behaviour. The ladies of the imperial household all got involved backing various bishops and sending in their personal guards to attack and beat up the opposing bishops. The final decision went in favour of Cyril and 'theotokos' passed into the doctrines of the church.

= Mary the 'God bearer'

At Chalcedon in 451 AD, 500 bishops gathered to accept six documents as oecumenical documents of the faith. This means all churches that considered themselves to be orthodox and catholic accepted these documents. This included the creeds of Nicaea and Constantinople. They were concerned to express unequivocally the tri-personality of the one Godhead, the true deity of the Son and the Spirit, the complete and permanent humanity united to the complete and permanent deity of the one Christ. The driving force behind the council was Leo the Bishop of Rome though he never attended in person but just sent his legates as his official representatives. The Emperor Marcion was very pro Leo and supported his role in the council.

Throughout this period, there were several key men of influence and power in the church who sought to keep the church doctrinally true to scripture. This was a period of controversy and disputes between the churches and their bishops that can only be described as disappointing. However, their influence has had a major impact on future generations. J.S. Lidell says, "*In passing to the West we leave behind the doctrine of the Fatherhood of God. Superficial and profound expressions of Western Religion replaced the Fatherhood of God with his sovereignty. These introduced legal considerations, which reacted with the doctrine of divine sovereignty, fixing it, filling it out, and connecting it with the doctrine of the church as the sphere and instrument of the earthly rule of God. All this happened without check, except for modifications introduced here and there by the warmth of a more evangelical faith, as, for example, in the case of Augustine himself"* (*Ibid*, p96.).

One of the new Latin leaders was Ambrose, the powerful and ambitious bishop of Milan (340 - 397). He was appointed bishop before he had been baptized as a Christian having arrived in Milan during the fighting caused by the election of a new bishop. Ambrose's strong personality and his armed guards made him the perfect candidate. As a result, he was quickly baptized, ordained and enthroned. He was bishop throughout the years when the emperors in the West were sympathetic to the Arians. He refused to be manipulated by them and withstood the attacks of the empress who massacred many orthodox Christians. He was a compassionate man and used church money to buy back prisoners taken by the Goths.

THE CAPPADOCIAN FATHERS
– THE LOVING RELATIONSHIP IN THE TRINITY

In the East, there were a number of leaders who were collectively referred to as the Cappadocian Fathers. They were Basil of Caesarea and his brother Gregory of Nyssa, and Gregory Nazianzus. These men were shining lights in a gradually dimming landscape. They carried the torch that Athanasius had lit a century before. Gregory Nazianzus, in particular like Athanasius, had a great emphasis on God as a Father.

For Gregory, the fact that God is called Father is basic to his understanding of the nature of God. He maintains that since God is called Father, he must have a Son from the same essence, but also that the Father must be the source of the Son and the Holy Spirit. Gregory understands the unity of the Trinity to come from God the Father, and the distinctness of the persons of the Trinity to be understood in the relational names of Father, Son and Holy Spirit. Since the three persons of the Trinity bear these three names, Gregory recognized and taught that they must be understood to stand in a certain relationship to one another. The trinity was about relationship in his thinking. Moreover, Gregory's view of a unified yet ordered Trinity, with the Father as its monarch, is crucial for his understanding of the way humanity relates with the Trinity.

Like Athanasius, Gregory's understanding of our salvation is dependent on the question of the relationship between the Father and the Son, but also on the question of the Father's relationship with the Holy Spirit. Gregory concludes, as Athanasius does of the Son, of Jesus, that if the Spirit is not fully divine, then he cannot participate in God's great work of salvation. Since the Spirit is part of the plan of salvation laid out in the scriptures, Gregory argues, to deny the Spirit full divinity is to put salvation in jeopardy.

Whilst this may appear academic, the issue at stake was the centrality of the nature of God as three persons in one and as fully divine and how they relate to us as sons. The Greek fathers of the church saw the Trinity as an expression of the loving relationship of the Godhead and that they relate to us as a loving relationship. The saving work of Jesus was based, first and foremost, on a loving relationship.

In the west, however, the language of theology was not Greek but Latin. Western leaders increasingly lost the ability to read and understand the language of the Eastern Churches and theologians. Misunderstandings of each other's language led to a loss of trust and a lack of clarity in communication.

Augustine of Hippo
– the Mastermind behind Western Theology

The most significant and influential of all the church Fathers in the West was Augustine of Hippo (354 - 430). He was to be an ongoing influence for centuries to come. He documents his conversion in his *Confessions* which tell a very modern-sounding story of a wildly rebellious youth, saved by the continual prayers of his mother and finally by the Lord speaking to him and telling him to get up and read. This took him to Romans 13:13-14. Before this, he had prayed on one occasion "Lord grant me chastity, but not yet!"

Augustine was probably the greatest mind since Paul. He became the most distinguished theologian of the early church, immersed in the letters of Paul, and teaching on the grace of God. He wrote an apology called *The City of God*. Augustine sought to combat the errors of Donatist rebaptism and as a result encouraged infant baptism. He also wrote extensively on the subject of the fall and original sin, the necessity of grace to free the will in turning to God and the predestination and perseverance of the 'fixed number of the elect'.

Augustine's rival in this respect was a British monk called Pelagius, who denied the need for grace to set the will in action, denied the concept of original sin, and believed in the possibility of sinlessness. Augustine came to Christ after deep and long conviction of sin and was overwhelmed with the knowledge of God's grace. Pelagius, on the other hand, was a devout monk who on arriving in Rome and seeing the lax morality of many Christians in the city was deeply concerned for righteousness.

The depth of Augustine's devotional life can be seen in the following quotation, *"Can any praise be worthy of the Lord's majesty? How magnificent his strength! How inscrutable his wisdom! Man is one of your creatures, Lord, and his instinct is to praise you. He bears about him the mark of death, the sign of his own sin, to remind him that you thwart the proud. But still, since he is part of your creation, he wishes to praise you. The thought of you stirs him so deeply that he cannot be content unless he praises you, because you made us for yourself and our hearts find no peace until they rest in you"* (Augustine, *Confessions*).

Augustine's doctrine of the trinity absolutely emphasized the equality of the three persons in the godhead. To Augustine, it was the holy trinity not specifically the Father who sent Jesus into the world. This meant that it was no longer God's Fatherhood that led to the actions of the Father, in the Son by the Spirit. Occasionally, Augustine spoke of God as Father, especially where the New Testament forced him to do so. Instead to Augustine, triune activity grew out of a sovereign and not a fatherly loving relationship. For Augustine, there is no thought that the sonship of Christ declares truth about the sonship of believers in and through him. Jesus' incarnation is not explained by relationship of Sonship at all. Rather, it is as a continuous act of humility, condescending to become a man, to serve and to suffer. Augustine sees this not as a response of the love of the Father in sending the Son rather it is a sign of obedience and trust by the Son.

The path on which Augustine set western Christianity would support the development of a legalistic and hierarchical church. His teaching on obedience and righteousness would pave the way for a view of God the Father who is distant and aloof, high above and disconnected from mankind whom he views with angry and righteous judgment. Where sin and the sinner has to be punished by an angry God who demands satisfaction for the offence caused by sin. He sets the course for the future where men are terrified of offending God, insecure about their status as Christians and driven to works to attain salvation.

Augustine's work on the *City of God*, along with the withdrawal to the east of the Roman emperors, would pave the way for the rise of the Pope as the most influential figure in the west. Thus, Catholicism superseded imperial Rome. In Augustine's theology, all the conditions were in place for substituting divine sovereignty for the loving Fatherhood of God. This model would rule the theology of the Middle Ages and dominate the thinking of the church.

Augustine died during the Vandal siege of Hippo in North Africa in 430 AD as the Roman world in the west collapsed about him.

Eastern Expansion and The Fall of Rome

In 315 AD, the Emperor Constantine had moved his capital to Byzantium in the east on the Bospherus where Europe touches Asia and renamed it Constantinople. The dynasty founded by Constantine was at best nominally Christian or worst, Arian. The family was torn apart with suspicion and many members were murdered or executed over the years. The East became the main centre of the Empire that flourished for many more centuries while the West began a steady decline. Imperial power waned in the West but the church increasingly began to fill the gap in authority and administration. The Bishop of Rome began taking on almost imperial powers over much of the lands in the West.

In the East, the Imperial City of Constantinople became a major centre not only for the Emperor, but also for its bishop or patriarch. The Patriarch began to assume great authority and prestige. Many obtained office through ambition and political maneuvering. One exception to this catalogue of unworthy holders of this position was John Chrysostom (347 - 407). He was an outstanding preacher who had chosen the monastic life but was ordained a presbyter in Antioch. His nickname was Golden Mouth – Chrysostom. While visiting the city, the Empress impressed with his preaching had him kidnapped and forced him to move to Constantinople in order to become its bishop in 398. John found the city full of vice and immorality and he refused to condone the corruption in the imperial court in Constantinople. This meant he soon fell victim to Empress Eudoxia who now opposed him. She got the support of the bishop of Alexandria to unseat John and as a result, he was exiled in 404. His final sermon before the Imperial family was based on the beheading of John the Baptist. He said, "Once again Salome dances, again Herodias rages; again she is confounded; again she demands the head of John on a charger." He was banished in 407 and was forced to keep walking until he died somewhere in the hills of Cappadocia.

In Rome, a young man named Jerome (346 - 420) who was a very gifted Latin scholar with amazing linguistic ability was extremely influential in the church. He was keenly attracted to the ascetic lifestyle and became a monk. He wrote many letters, but was increasingly critical of the decadence he saw around him in the fading city. He left Rome in 386 and settled in Bethlehem where he founded a monastery. His greatest contribution was that he translated the Bible into Latin. This translation is known as the Vulgate. This became the approved translation for the Roman Catholic Church in the West for the next 1500 years. His translation was, however, influenced by his theology. For example, it was Jerome who changed the brothers of Jesus into cousins in order to protect the idea of the perpetual virginity of the Blessed Virgin Mary. Virginity had become a mark of spirituality to many and had been applied to Mary some time before.

Throughout this period, missionary expansion continued to take place within the empire and beyond. In 301 AD, King Tiridates proclaimed Christianity as the sole religion in Armenia making that nation-state the second in history to declare itself Christian. The growing Barbarian threat along all the borders was no barrier to the gospel. A monk called Ulfilas evangelised among the Goths in Germany and along the northern borders of the empire. The Bible was translated into Gothic in 340 AD. Ethiopia was evangelised by Athanasius who preached and established churches there every time he was sent into exile from Alexandria. A monk called Ninian christianised Scotland, beyond the Roman wall in the north of Britannia around 395. The Celtic Church became a missionary base that reached out to the Welsh, the Irish and the Picts. Many of the Barbarian races became Arian and later converted to orthodox Christianity.

After the banishment of Nestorius in 431, he took the gospel to China were a Nestorian church survived for the next five hundred years.

The Barbarian tribes that pressed in upon the northern borders of the empire finally overwhelmed the weakened western half of the empire in the beginning of the fifth century. The legions were withdrawn from Britain in 400 as the Saxons, Angles and Jutes poured across the North Sea. The Visigoths and Ostrogoths overwhelmed the Goths who settled in Gaul.

When the Visigoths sacked Rome in 410, the psychological shock waves shook the whole world. The Western Emperor had withdrawn to the safety of the marshes in Ravenna and Rome was left to the Goths and the church. It was the end of an era. The Vandals swept into Spain and North Africa. Augustine died during the Vandal siege of Hippo that fell in 430. Saxons, Jutes and Angles overran Britain. Gaul fell to the Franks and Allemani. Attila the Hun swept through Western Europe in 452 and was prevented from sacking Rome by the intercession of the Pope. The Eastern Empire was not as weak as the west and survived the onslaught, though it was challenged on all sides.

MONASTICISM - CHRISTIAN ESCAPISM

The Christian reaction to the collapse of the western empire was to retreat into Monasticism. This had been growing in influence for several generations, as a reaction against what some felt was the growing power of the organised church and its hierarchical structure. Its rise was not documented but the evidence of its emergence is clearly seen.

As early as 251 AD, a man called Anthony living in Egypt retreated into the desert to fight the flesh and worldliness. Basil of Caesarea claims he was the first monk. Many others took up this approach. Pachomius (292 - 346) founded communities of monks in Egypt. Initially, it was a strongly eastern movement and was escapist in the sense that it provided a religious escape route from the corruption and immorality of late Roman society. Throughout the fourth century, numerous communities were founded in the east. By the early fifth century, monks and monk scholars dominated the Eastern Church. In an attempt to retreat completely from the world, some even climbed on top of pillars living there for years. They were known as pillar saints. Simon Stylites, being the most famous, lived atop his column in Syria for years. All manner of strange behaviour was practiced in the guise of monastic devotion. One man, John the dwarf, apparently watered a dry stick daily for three years as an expression of obedience. Another, Simeon the Holy Fool, pretended madness to hide his acts of charity, which explains why he dragged a dead dog around with him.

Jerome in Rome and Martin of Tours in Gaul championed Western Monasticism at the end of the fourth century. The Celtic Church partly due to its isolation was strongly monastic. Ninian, Patrick (c389 - c461) and Columba (c521 - 597) were leading figures. The Celtic church kept the gospel alive in the north and west of the British Isles long after the Romans had abandoned Britain. Their monasteries and churches became centres of learning and art. They copied and illustrated beautiful manuscripts and books such as the Lindisfarne Gospels and the Book of Kells. From his base on Iona, Columba led missions into Northumbria. There were numerous accounts of healings that were attributed to these early Celtic monks and missionaries.

Monasticism's greatest early leader was Benedict of Nursia who founded a monastery at Monte Cassino in Italy in 525. His followers became known as Benedictine Monks and follow the Rule of Benedict, which was a handbook of instructions for living the life of a monk.

The Eastern Empire was very different. The empire remained strong and underwent a resurgence of culture under strong emperors such as Justinian (483 - 565) who reconquered North Africa, Sicily and Southern Italy from the Vandals and Goths. He built the huge church of Santa Sophia in Constantinople and encouraged the spread of Byzantinian culture and architecture across the empire. He called together the theologians in councils in order to "deal with" heretics such as the Montanists. The Code of Justinian became the legal and religious code of the Eastern Church for the next 1000 years.

The so-called barbarian tribes that overwhelmed most of the western empire in the fourth century were either total pagans or Arian and therefore were considered heretics. These barbarian tribes, notably the Ostrogoths in Italy and the Vandals in North Africa, ruthlessly persecuted 'Catholic' Christians. They now occupied most of the old Western Roman Empire. The Frankish kingdom in Gaul was ruled by King Clovis (466 - 515) who became Catholic when his Christian wife Clotilde persuaded him to convert. With the support of the Roman Church, most of "France" came under Frankish Christian control. Theodoric the Ostrogoth (455 - 526), the Arian King of Italy was remarkably tolerant of other groups. His close friend and consul Boethius, known as "The Last of the Romans", was a Catholic who together with Theodoric brought a period of prosperity to ravaged Italy.

THE RISE OF THE PAPACY

Throughout this early period, the church in Rome at the centre of the Empire claimed precedence over other churches by virtue of Rome being the capital city. The first list of Roman bishops appeared as early as 160 - 185. They name Peter and Paul jointly as co-founders of the Roman church. In 220, Bishop Callistus recognised Peter as the first bishop of Rome. Rome was the only church in the west that could claim to be founded by an apostle. Over the years, the bishop of Rome exploited this claim to apostolic foundation.

Constantine's support for the church in Rome added to its prestige and its wealth. By the mid fourth century, there were forty church buildings in Rome. After the Council of Constantinople in 381, Damasus of Rome declared that the Roman church owed its primacy not to decrees of a council, but to the powers committed to Peter by Christ. Therefore, the Bishop of Rome claimed it was the apostolic see without qualification.

Siricius (384 - 399) began to refer to himself as the father of the church calling himself papa. Over time, this became the term Pope. He also called himself to be the heir of Peter. Various claims by bishops in Rome in the next few years were rejected by the Eastern churches but generally accepted by the Western churches. For example, Innocent I in 415 AD declared, *"Whatever is done in the provinces should not be taken as concluded until it has come to the knowledge of this see."*

Leo The Great, who was Pope from 440 – 461, stayed in Rome when all other authority had fled. He increased the authority of the Roman church extending its control over all the churches in the West claiming to be the true successor to Peter and calling himself the Universal Bishop. Though again, the Eastern Church rejected this. Rome became a "Christian" City under his rule.

Gregory the Great (540 - 604) was elected Pope in 590 and was the first of the Medieval Popes. He effectively assumed temporal responsibility for much of central Italy as well as spiritual responsibility. He promoted the Benedictine Monks and encouraged their missionary activity. He sent one of his monks, Augustine to England to convert the Angles. After asking about origins of some Angle slaves he saw in the market of Rome, he declared that hence forth they should not be Angles but Angels, thus inventing the first English pun. He reorganized the liturgy and taught Gregorian chants. He saw the papacy as the successors to

Peter and the supreme authority in the church. He titled himself the Vicar of Christ on earth.

The idea of apostolic succession was first hinted at by Clement, Bishop of Rome at the end of the first century. In seeking to defend the church from heresy, however, he spoke of a plurality of bishops, and did not pull rank on bishops from other cities. Later, in the third century, the issue of rebaptism led to conflict between Cyprian, Bishop of Carthage and Stephen, Bishop of Rome, who were claiming pre-eminence among all other bishops. By the fourth century, the dominance of the Bishop of Rome had been established. Pope Damasus (304–384) established the new order. He was the first to refer to other bishops as sons instead of brothers. He attained the position of Pope in 366 AD by defeating a rival in a church riot, where over a hundred lives were lost. To overcome the evident weakness of his moral authority, he emphasised the exalted spiritual dignity of his office and began to adorn the tombs of martyrs and popes. The opulence of the papal entertainments was thought to surpass the heights of imperial hospitality. The Bishop of Rome referred to himself as the Father or Papa of the church, hence the Pope. The church had become a man made institution dominated by an orphan spirited hierarchy.

When the Romans abandoned Britain in 410 AD, the Celtic Church was separated from the Roman Church by a sea of barbarians. The new settlers in Britain were Angles and Saxons hence the name Anglo Saxon to describe the English. The Celtic church survived in the north and in the western isles of Scotland and Ireland and led the way in converting the English.

I have mentioned already that Pope Gregory on seeing blond slaves in

Rome in 596 sent Augustine to England. Landing in Kent in 597 AD, he began to preach. King Ethelbert of Kent was married to a Christian princess Bertha of Paris and he insisted that the whole kingdom become Christian. Augustine built his first church in Canterbury, the Kentish capital. The Anglo Saxon Church in the south looked to Canterbury and Rome. The North of Britain was Celtic and led by Aiden whose centre was Lindisfarne. York was also an important centre. At the Synod of Whitby in 664, the two churches merged and adopted the Roman traditions including the correct form of haircuts for monks.

The English Church was strongly evangelistic and English missionaries went out preaching. Wilfrid, Bishop of York converted the south Saxons on the Isle of Wight. Willibrord went to Frisia in 690 and Winfrith, known as Boniface (680 - 753) to Thuringia and Bavaria.

THE RISE AND ONSLAUGHT OF ISLAM

Whilst all this was happening in the west, there was a growing sense of nationalism in the Arabian Peninsula among the local Arab tribes. In 570, Muhammad was born in Mecca. His father died before he was born. At the age of six, Muhammad lost his mother and became an orphan. He was subsequently brought up for two years under the guardianship of his paternal grandfather. When he was eight years of age, his grandfather also died. Muhammad now came under the care of his uncle. Muhammad's guardians saw that he did not starve to death, but it was hard for them to do more for him, especially as the fortunes of the clan of Hashim seemed to have been declining at that time. He was an orphan in every sense of the word.

He grew up knowing mainly heretical Christians and seeing virtual idolatry in the worship of saints and martyrs and adoration of images and icons. Following revelations supposedly from the angel Gabriel, he led a group of 200 followers into exile from Mecca in 622. In the desert, he refined his beliefs and returned in 631 to Mecca a hero and great religious teacher. Within a year, the whole of Arabia followed his teaching. He was fiercely pro Arab and violently anti Christian whom he saw as idolaters. His nationalism brought him and his new religion into conflict with Greek, Roman, and Byzantinian culture. His followers armed themselves and started to spread the teaching of Islam, which means submission. They moved with their armies northeast and west into the lands of the old Roman and Persian empires.

Within one hundred years, Islam reigned from the Atlantic to India. It was the end of the dominance of Christianity in North Africa. Islamic policy was conversion by the sword. The people of the lands they conquered had to convert or be killed. Ten thousand churches were destroyed in Syria alone. By the eleventh century, only five churches remained in North Africa. Carthage fell in 697. The great centres at Alexandria, Jerusalem and Antioch were also wiped out. Constantinople was attacked in 670. By 715, most of Spain had fallen and by 732, the Muslims were at the gates of Poitiers in France. It was the twilight of the Eastern Church. Small, resolute but persecuted minorities of Christians hung on in all these lands right into the twenty-first century where again today they are being persecuted by a militant form of Islam.

The Church after 700 years

It is appropriate at this point to pause and look at the state of Christianity by the year 700. Primitive New Testament Christianity had become Medieval Catholicism in the West and Eastern Orthodoxy in the East. The Lord's Supper had become a ritual sacrifice re-enacted on an altar, known as the Mass. Confession before the mass became compulsory for all as a control factor. Penance, that is the self-atoning for sin in various ways was widely practised. Incense originally used to deodorise the smelly barbarians became part of the ritual. Purgatory in the afterlife was believed to be a place where one worked off unconfessed sin and atoned for failure that happened in this life. Infant baptism was the normal practice.

Prayers for the dead that they might be quickly removed from purgatory became a feature of catholic practice. Prayers were offered to the departed saints and were widely practised. This received official Papal sanction in 787. There was widespread belief that the prayers of people alive on earth could assist people in getting out of purgatory. Adoration of and prayers to Mary, images and icons were part of every church. Places of worship became "holy" and copied the pagan practice of adornment. The priests copied the pagan pattern with vestments and were required to be celibate and unmarried. There was a professional class of clergy distinct from the laity. Monasticism became an escape route from everyday life and was seen as more spiritual and a sure route to heaven. Papal claims sought to reinforce the position of the bishop of Rome who was viewed as the head of the church in the West. Papal authority became immense in the wake of the fall of the Roman Empire, with an enormous bureaucracy and chain of command.

The church had lost salvation by faith in the sacrificial death of Jesus and his redemption of us on the cross. This had been replaced with insecurity and the only alternative consisted in various types of works and legalistic religious practice. The church had lost the Holy Spirit as the giver of life and power to individuals. God the Father had become the angry judge who was distant and demanded retribution and satisfaction. Man appeased God's wrath through works and religious duty. God's Fatherhood whilst described theologically was in reality replaced by his absolute and arbitrary sovereignty. Sonship was a completely unknown concept. New Testament Christianity as it had been did not exist anywhere.

Political influences mixed with the legalism of Roman religion led to an interpretation of God's relationship with mankind in terms of law. The creeds became laws imposed by authority. The Medieval conscience was continually reminded of the presence of a divine Judge who was embodied in the rule of the Papacy. This led to the introduction of Church law or Canon law in the thirteenth century. The study of law passed into the life of the church. To be a leading figure in the church was to be a jurist and arbiter of law. God gradually was distanced from everyone and his representative on earth, his vicar, was the pope and the church hierarchy.

CHAPTER SEVEN

Darkness and a Slow Dawning of Light 700 - 1500

The years between 700 and about 1000 are known as the Dark Ages partly because of the decline in civilization in the old western empire. The loss of so much knowledge, including for many the ability to read or write, meant that little is recorded from those years. The east however retained much of this ability and the flowering of Islamic culture was anything but dark. Yet, our perspective from a twenty-first century Western viewpoint is that these were the Dark Ages.

There were however seasons of recovery and development, from time to time, but this was not widespread. There was a period of revival in the Frankish church that took place under their king Charles Martel. He defeated the Muslims in France at Poitiers in 732 halting their advancement in Western Europe. King Martel founded the Carolingian Dynasty and on his death his son Pepin (714 – 768) made alliances with the Pope supporting him against the attacks of the invading tribe the Lombards, in Italy. Significantly, he gave the Pope lands to rule in central Italy. This elevated the Pope from being just a spiritual leader to a temporal ruler. "The Donation of Constantine" appeared at this time that claimed to be a letter from the Emperor Constantine giving all of Western Europe to the Pope to rule. This proved to be a totally fake document.

Pepin's son, Charlemagne (742 – 814) was crowned in 800 by Pope Leo III. He gave him the title Holy Roman Emperor and his lands were titled the Holy Roman Empire. In reality, it was not remotely 'Holy', nor was it 'Roman' or an empire. However, it was a time of renewed activity in church building, literature and the arts. Beautiful manuscripts were produced and universities and education began to be developed around monasteries. Charlemagne's military success included pushing the Muslims down into southern Spain and extending his empire into Bavaria, Saxony and Pannonia. Saxons converted en masse to Christianity at the point of a sword. Those who refused conversion were beheaded. However, his empire fragmented after his death and was divided up into smaller kingdoms under the unfortunately named Holy Roman Emperor, Charles the Fat in 887.

The ninth and tenth centuries were a time of total chaos in Europe as climate change led to population explosions in Scandinavia. Vikings and Norsemen poured into northern Europe destroying all in their path. The Celtic church virtually ceased to exist before the onslaught. Arabs advanced into Sicily, Crete and Southern Italy. Magyars migrating westward from the steppes of Russia overwhelmed Hungary in the late ninth century. Persecutions broke out in China in 845 and all evidence of Christianity was gone by 987.

The 'conversion' of the Slavs and Bulgars happened during 850 to 900. The conversion of Moravia occurred when King Rastiz declared those who would not become Christians would be strangled. Poland was Christianized by 968 AD and the Magyars in Hungary by 973. Most of the Northmen's kingdoms became Christian by the end of the first millennium. The terms Christian and conversion are very loose terms in this era.

Powerful Roman families controlled the Papacy in Italy. Anarchy and vice were legendary in the Papal household. There were three rival popes at one point and possibly even a female one masquerading as a man. Clerical ignorance was such that many were illiterate and the common people did not understand the liturgy. Church jobs went to the highest bidder or the best-connected family.

The Russian Emperor Vladimir converted to Orthodox Christianity in 988 and opened up his whole empire to Byzantine Orthodox missionaries. The Slavic languages were imposed on these churches rather than Greek though the style of the new churches was eastern and orthodox rather than western and catholic.

The final split between the Eastern Orthodox Church and the Western Roman Catholic Church occurred in 1054 following centuries of growing tension and disagreement. The Pope excommunicated the Patriarch of Constantinople and vice versa and the breach continues to this day, though they are at least talking.

PAPAL CORRUPTION AND THE HORROR OF THE CRUSADES.

The papacy reached the height of its temporal power in the next few centuries. Pope Gregory VII on becoming pope in 1073 set out to become the most powerful man in the world. He established a College of Cardinals who fulfilled many of the secular functions within the

Papal States. He sought to control the Holy Roman Emperor and thereby dominate Europe. Pope Alexander III in 1177 had the Emperor Frederick Barbarossa groveling on his knees seeking forgiveness. Henry II of England was dealt with similarly following the murder of Thomas a Becket, the Archbishop of Canterbury in 1178. Innocent III, Pope from 1198 - 1216 imposed his rule over King John of England by forcing him to accept a different Archbishop of Canterbury. The temporal power of the papacy was huge. At the fourth Lateran Council in 1215, the doctrine of transubstantiation of the mass was made official in which it was taught that the bread and wine were literally transformed into the actual body and blood of Christ.

Boniface VIII, pope from 1294 to 1303, struggled to retain power over strong kings in France and Spain so he made the following doctrine official, *"Every human creature is to be subject to the Roman Pontiff and this is altogether necessary for salvation."* By 1302, Pope Boniface said in Papal Bull Unam Sanctum *"that which was spoken of Christ, 'thou hast subdued all things under his feet,' may well be verified in me. I have the authority of the King of Kings. I am all in all and above all so that God himself and I, the vicar of God have but one consistory, and I am able to do almost all that God can do. What therefore can you make of me but God?"*

However by the fourteenth century, the strife between kings and princes across Europe involving a great deal of military as well as political activity weakened the Pope's influence. The King of France forced the Papacy to move from Rome to Avignon where the Pope came under the protection of the France from 1309 to 1377 and were effectively, puppets of the French kings. Meanwhile, rival popes were installed in Rome from 1378 to 1417.

One possible way of escape to a more spiritual climate was to join a monastery, and in this period, many thousands of men and women chose this way of life. Some monastic orders saw themselves as missionaries taking the gospel to new places, but the majority of monasteries remained inward looking. The concept of withdrawal has its root in other religions and Gnosticism, with the erroneous view that the flesh was basically evil and had to be suppressed for the sake of the soul. A first expression of this spirit was for individuals to live as hermits, often in the desert under extreme conditions. Then groups of like-minded men would live together in ill-defined communities, culminating in the major monastic orders with clearly defined rules of routine and discipline. Large numbers of men and women joined such orders as the Benedictines (founded in 529), Cistercians (1098), who numbered Bernard of Clairvaux among its ranks, Carmelites (1209), Augustinians (1244), and the preaching orders of Dominicans (1216) and Franciscans (1223) founded by the saintly and godly Francis of Assisi.

There were benefits for the Church in that the monastic life proved a strong resistance to worldliness, promoted theological and other academic study, and provided food and help for the outcasts of society. At the same time, the system withdrew men and women from involvement in society, encouraged pride and hypocrisy, promoted across the Christian world wrong ideas about faith and morality, and served to reinforce the hierarchical nature of the church. The Knights Templar who were a cross between soldiers and monks were founded in 1118 to defend Jerusalem. They are now associated with the nonsensical belief in the search for the mythical Holy Grail.

Inquisition

The Dominicans, also known as the Black Friars, founded in 1215 were referred to as "The Lord's Watchdogs" since they were staunch theologians and were encouraged to seek out and purge heresy. They became the main promoters of the notorious Inquisition. Thomas Aquinas (1224–1274), well known philosopher and theologian, was a Dominican. Aquinas is famous for his extremely lengthy doctrinal work and amongst other things the debate over how many angels can dance on a pinhead. Aquinas and Anselm (1033 – 1109), the English theologian and Archbishop of Canterbury, are known as the Schoolmen. These Schoolmen, particularly Anselm, developed Augustinian theology and codified doctrine into Canon law. The church at this time was legalistic and cold. Their works are not bedtime reading.

This was also the age of the great European cathedrals and abbeys that were built throughout the Middle Ages. The notion was to create awesome buildings that soared heavenwards that were seen in themselves as a witness to God's grandeur and majesty and a sign of the church's might and power.

When the Seljuck Turks captured Jerusalem from the Arabs, Christian pilgrims were banned from the holy sites. The Holy Land and the holy places now lay in the hands of the Saracens, and almost in the spirit of the Islamic holy war, it became the duty of all good Christians to go out and win these places back from the infidels. This was a major tragedy of the Middle Ages with countless atrocities committed in the name of Christ upon Muslims and Jews in Palestine and across the Levant.

Crusades

Between 1095 and 1291, at least ten major crusades were launched for this purpose, some of them mobilizing up to a million fighting men. Most ended in total disaster with none of the objectives accomplished. 90% of the 275,000 who set out on the first crusade died in the process. The most tragic was the Children's Crusade of 1212 in which the twenty thousand children who set out either died on the way or were sold into slavery. The popes had granted plenary indulgences to all who took part. A plenary indulgence was the forgiveness of sins that an individual had committed before the grant and also any sins committed on the crusade. This opened up the door for crusaders to slaughter and rape at will on crusade. Horrific atrocities were committed across the Middle East as a result. The prisons of Europe were opened and some of the worst criminals were encouraged to join the crusades. It is not surprising that under this license, the crusaders did terrible harm to innocent citizens on their way, to Orthodox Christians, Muslims and to the Jews in the Holy Land. This has damaged the reputation of the Christian church in the Muslim world ever since. This was not the church's finest hour.

Lights Amid the Darkness

There were, however, throughout the Dark Ages some godly individuals who sought to be true to a Christian value system. They are hard to find but they were there. The Venerable Bede (673 – 735) in Northumbria and Alfred the Great (849 – 899), the Saxon king are examples of saintly men in England in these dark years. The vice and corruption in many monastic communities was shocking. Then a form of renewed spiritual life began in Cluny in 910 when Duke William of Aquitaine founded a monastery that influenced many existing monasteries and led to a reemphasis of spirituality.

English Monks undertook the conversion of Scandinavia during the eleventh century and much of northern Europe was Christianized. In the 1100s, Hildegard of Bingen (1098 – 1179) founded a convent and was the first woman noted as having composed music. She wrote theological, botanical, and medicinal texts, as well as letters, liturgical songs, poems, and the first surviving morality play, while supervising brilliant miniature illuminations in manuscripts. She is reputed to have spoken and sung in tongues. Contemporaries who heard her spiritual songs referred to them as "concerts in the Spirit".

Francis of Assisi was a similar light amid the darkness. His godly life inspired many of his contemporaries to a simpler lifestyle of poverty, chastity and service to the poor. He was an effective preacher and is now widely recognised by many as an outstanding example of living a courageous Christian life. One of his many recorded quotes was "Preach the gospel every day and if necessary, use words."

In spite of these examples, the prevailing view of the dark ages and medieval church life is predominately depressing. However, in this turbulent and contradictory period of church history, there were stirrings across Europe in the shape of non-conformist groups and individuals who resisted the prevailing mood and sought to live lives based on biblical revelation. It is difficult to know much about them because the only information available comes from their enemies, as the church viewed them as heretical in their day. Sometimes through their ignorance of the Scriptures and lack of education and teaching they embraced wrong ideas, but all were prepared to die for their beliefs.

As early as the seventh century, a group known as Paulicians rejected papal claims of authority. In their book, *The Key of Truth,* they taught repentance, faith and water baptism of believers. Needless to say, they were considered heretics by the church and by 867 had been wiped out.

Another group known as the Bogomils emerged in tenth century Bulgaria. They were condemned for refusing to worship Mary and Icons but also had a variety of confused doctrines that could be connected to Gnosticism.

The Albigenses were the most well known of these groups. They were also known as Cathars, emerging in southern France in the thirteenth century. They had similar ideas to the Bogomils and were characterized by a strong rejection of Papal claims and much of the popular Catholicism of the day. Their theology was muddled and probably unbiblical in many areas but their passion and zeal for what they perceived was truth was exemplary. They believed that all Christians needed to be baptized as believers and receive the 'Consolamentum' that was essentially the baptism of the Holy Spirit. Pope Innocent III sent the English knight Simon De Montfort on a crusade to persecute these so called heretical groups. There were scenes of horrific and wholesale slaughter in southern France. Underlying this was a growing recognition that Catholicism of the late middle Ages was unlike Biblical Christianity in almost every way.

In the late twelfth century, a Frenchman in Lyon, Peter Waldo (1140 - c1218) founded a group that began as a spiritual movement within the church. Waldo began to preach and teach on the streets based on his ideas of simplicity and poverty. Notably, that "No man can serve two masters, God and mammon." By 1170, he had gathered a number of followers and they started to be called *the Poor of Lyon, the Poor of Lombardy*, or *the Poor of God*. They were also referred to as the Waldensians after their leader.

The Waldensian movement was characterised from the beginning by lay preaching, voluntary poverty and sticking to the "Word of God", the Bible. Peter Waldo commissioned a cleric from Lyons around 1180 to translate the Bible, or parts of it, into the Provencal language. A traveling

Waldensian preacher was known as a *barba* and could be either man or woman. The idea of a female preacher was novel, almost revolutionary in and of itself, for the era. The group would shelter and house the *barba* and help make arrangements to move them on to the next town in secret.

Driven away from Lyon, Waldo and his followers settled in the high valleys of Piedmont and in France, in the Luberon and in the Alpine regions of Europe where they could escape the attentions of bishops. Finally, Pope Lucius III excommunicated Waldo during the synod held at Verona. The doctrine of the Poor of Lyon was again condemned by the Fourth Lateran Council in 1215 and regarded as heresy. The Roman church began to persecute the Waldensians, and many were tried and sentenced to death in various European countries during the twelfth, thirteenth, and fourteenth centuries. Those who survived did so by retreating into the high Alpine valleys. Centuries after Waldo's death, the Waldensian denomination joined the Genevan or Reformed branch of the Protestant Reformation.

John Wycliffe –
Morning Star of the Reformation

John Wycliffe (1320–1384), a scholarly Oxford don, was appalled by the corruption in the church. More than any other, John Wycliffe prepared the ground for the coming reformation of the sixteenth century. He saw the idolatry that was encouraged by practices in the Mass and strongly advocated a return to Scripture and following the way of Christ. His most notable achievement was the first translation of the Bible from the Latin Vulgate into English in 1380. In an earlier book, *Of the Truth of Holy Scripture*, he had declared, "*The Bible is the word of God*"; "*Scripture is infallible; all other teachers, even Augustine, can lead to error*". He believed that the Pope, the Church Councils, and the Church Fathers only become authoritative if what they said agreed with Scripture. This was an astonishing statement after 1000 years of darkness in the church. The political implications of Wycliffe's radical ideas were taken up by popular preachers like John Ball and resulted in the Peasants' Revolt of 1377 to 1381. The revolt was put down with severity and Wycliffe's teaching discredited by association. In the reigns of Henry IV and V, it was a punishable offence to be found reading the Bible in English. Wycliffe's first priority was to provide the Scriptures in English for use by the clergy. He wanted to show the truth of the Bible as opposed to the common practices of the church as the basis of Christianity.

Wycliffe's influence was immense in the fifteenth century. Various groups emerged that had a lot in common in their beliefs, challenging papal authority with respect to the Bible, arguing for the inclusion of the laity in taking the wine in communion, amongst other issues. Many of these teachings stemmed from the teaching of John Wycliffe.

Immediately following the death of Wycliffe in 1384, a strong movement arose of people who were prepared to come out of the church for the principles that they hoped would have been accepted within. They became known as The Lollards, or babblers. They preached a gospel that saw Christ as the sole head of the church. They looked to the authority of Scripture alone for direction. They saw communion as a remembrance and proclamation of the death of Christ rather than the reenactment of his death by the priests. They also opposed the corruption of the organised church. A Lollard statement of 1394 said, "*We ask God then of his supreme goodness to reform our church as being entirely out of joint to the perfectness of its first beginnings.*"

The movement gained much support in England, including some of the nobility, a number of merchants, tradesmen and artisans and many peasants. A Catholic observer of the time commented that if you ever saw two men walking along a road, at least one would be a Wycliffist or Lollard. However, this popular movement was suppressed by Henry IV who passed an law in 1400 banning the schools, books and preaching of the Lollards and providing for the arrest, trial, and possible execution of those who professed this teaching. After a number of trials and executions around the country, the movement was driven to secrecy and by 1431 the authorities considered the 'heresy' exterminated. How wrong they were!

Over in continental Europe, John Hus (1369 – 1415) was a Czech religious thinker, philosopher, reformer, and master at Charles University in Prague. He was deeply influenced by Wycliffe's writings. His followers became known as Hussites. The Roman Catholic Church considered his teachings heretical. Hus was excommunicated in 1411, then condemned by the Council of Constance, and burned at the stake in 1415. This caused considerable resentment in Bohemia and Moravia. The authorities of both countries appealed urgently to Sigismund, Holy Roman Emperor and repeatedly urged him to release Hus. When news of his death arrived, disturbances broke out, directed primarily against the clergy, especially against the monks. Even the archbishop of Prague narrowly escaped with his life from the effects of this popular anger. The treatment of Hus was felt to be a disgrace inflicted upon the whole country and his death was seen as a criminal act. This reaction by German kings and princes prepared the way for further resistance to Papal authority a century later.

THE RENAISSANCE – THE REBIRTH OF KNOWLEDGE

Meanwhile in northern Europe, notably in Holland, a spiritual renewal was taking place within the church. A new emphasis was being given to personal devotion to Christ. This can be best illustrated by the title of the devotional classic of this period by the Dutch Augustinian, Thomas a Kempis (1380–1471). The work is widely known as *The Imitation of Christ* but in fact its full title is *The Imitation of Christ and Contempt for the World*. It is a deeply spiritual and heart focused work. One such quote from this work says, "*If you want to have true delight, here is the way: have contempt for all worldly things and all lower delights, and rich consolation will, in turn, be given to you.*"

All across Europe there was a stirring in people's hearts to get back to a more biblical approach to the Christian faith. They were tired of the corrupt ways and lax living of many of the clergy and monks. They resented the demands made by the Roman Church on their money. It seemed there was a dawn coming of new light.

When Constantinople fell to the Turks in 1454, it marked the end of an era. It was the end of the Eastern Roman Empire that had survived for a thousand years after the fall of the western empire. The Eastern Orthodox Church that had its centre and patriarch in Constantinople now came under a period of domination by the Turks who were Muslims. Before the fall of the city, many Greek-speaking scholars and monks had fled to the west bringing with them numerous ancient manuscripts and books. The rediscovery of the Scriptures in their original languages was a major boost to the growing interest in the ancient world that marked the new learning and rebirth of knowledge that was happening in the newly emerging universities of Europe. This move is referred to as the Renaissance. This hunger for knowledge and learning was beginning to change the face of Europe.

In the last few years of the fifteenth century, Europe was a place of great excitement. It was a time of opportunity when new horizons were opening up almost everywhere. Among these were long sea voyages of discovery such as that of Columbus in 1492 that brought knowledge of new lands across the Atlantic, suggesting new worlds to be explored. Vasco da Gama's voyages to the East around the Cape of Good Hope in southern Africa and on to India in 1498 opened the east up again to Europe. A church was discovered on the east coast of India that traced its heritage back to the Apostle Thomas.

A major technological breakthrough happened in the invention of printing in 1450 by William Caxton starting a revolution in distributing information. Then there was a new realism in art and sculpture expressed through the genius of the likes of Leonardo da Vinci and Michelangelo to name but two. There was renewed interest in Greek language, philosophy and Roman authors from the classical era. Astronomical discoveries by Copernicus, Kepler, and Galileo began to challenge the received scientific views of the day. Up until this point, science was the preserve of the church alone, which is why Galileo's work was considered heretical rather than unscientific. However, it was a time for the opening up of minds. There was much to stimulate and the assurance of new territories to be explored, new discoveries to be made, new technologies, and new works of art. There was the prospect of one of the most creative periods in the history of mankind.

In comparison with the world around it, the church had little to offer. Inside the church, there was large-scale negligence and corruption. If you cared about your soul and its inevitable doom to purgatory and worse, which of course everyone did, you could earn time remission by purchasing an indulgence. Indulgences where supposed to be a treasury of the good deeds of Christ and the saints that could, if appropriated, offset time in purgatory. The Pope was the custodian of this merit and offered it in exchange for cash. This was essentially a chance to buy your way out of purgatory and the revenue from these sales made the church and its leaders very rich. As an alternative, you could abandon the world and join a monastery, but even that was not a passport to heaven as some were finding out and starting to challenge.

Humanism had begun to grip the educated classes during the Renaissance. Increased urbanization, the growth of universities and the invention of printing coupled with the spiritual bankruptcy of the church led many to question the whole medieval approach to church life.

A former Augustinian monk and great scholar in Rotterdam, Desiderius Erasmus (1466 – 1536) is regarded as the last 'pre-reformation' man. He encouraged the translation and printing of Latin and Greek texts to obtain accurate versions of the Scriptures. As a leading humanist concerned for the development of the individual, he urged a return to Scripture as the best guide to life. He wrote *The Handbook of the Christian Soldier* in 1503 as the layperson's guide to Scripture and practical morality. He advocated personal faith and conduct as opposed to reliance on priests. His influence as a humanist had a great impact on Sir Thomas More (1478 – 1536) in London who was Chancellor to King Henry VIII.

As great hunger for genuine spiritual life was growing across the whole of Europe, God was on the move and raised up a man to face the challenge. It was the beginning of a restoration to true biblical values that continues to this day.

CHAPTER EIGHT

The Reformation – The Rediscovery of Jesus

MARTIN LUTHER

In November 1483 in central Germany, a boy named Martin Luther was born to Saxon parents. He attended Erfurt University in 1501 and following a frightening encounter with lightning in a storm he vowed to St. Anne that he would become a monk if she spared his life. This was typical behaviour for the late Middle Ages. As a result, he became an Augustinian monk at the age of nineteen. He had an exceptional intellect, but a troubled conscience that made him a melancholic and depressive individual. To find peace with God, he had become a monk, but quickly discovered that however many spiritual exercises and acts of self-denial he undertook, his conscience only became more troubled.

In 1510, Martin Luther visited Rome for '*four weeks of steady disillusionment*'. He had entered the monastic life in an earnest attempt to find peace with God and personal assurance of salvation, and was confronted with the harsh reality that the church was in no state to offer him either. He returned home and became a professor at Wittenberg

University where he began to preach and teach through Paul's letter to the Romans. It was here that he came to grapple with Paul's words *'For in the gospel a righteousness from God is revealed, a righteousness that is by faith from first to last'* (Romans 1:17). A light went on in his heart and revelation came to him. He wrote, *"When I realised this I felt myself absolutely born again."*

The issue that brought Luther onto the stage of history was the selling of indulgences. Pope Leo X was attempting to raise money for the rebuilding of St. Peter's church in Rome. The old basilica built a thousand years before was crumbling into ruins and the Pope had great plans for a magnificent replacement. But the Pope was apparently short of cash for the job. So Pope Leo and the Roman church had offered a plenary indulgence in exchange for cash contributions. This meant anyone who paid a fee could buy a full "get out of purgatory card" which covered all your sins ever committed to date. Not only was this possible for yourself but also all your poor relatives who were suffering in purgatory. The fee payable was per individual so the opportunity to raise huge sums of money was limitless. Luther found the practice of selling indulgences utterly offensive. It produced a false sense of security of sins forgiven and was widely used by the church to unscrupulously raise money. Nowhere was this more so than in the hands of a Dominican monk by the name of Tetzel who was given the authority to sell indulgences around Germany. Tetzel's tactics were extreme manipulation of people's fears and superstitions. His sales jingle was, *"As soon as the coin in the coffer rings, the soul from purgatory springs!"* When he arrived in Wittenberg, Luther was incensed. Luther began to write a list of reasons why the selling of indulgences by the Pope was wrong. He came up with ninety-five reasons such as, if the Pope has the power to release people from purgatory why doesn't he just do it out of the kindness of his heart, or words to that effect.

On the eve of All Saints' Day, 31 October 1517, Luther nailed his 95 Theses against indulgences to the church door of the Castle Church at Wittenberg and so began the controversy that became the Reformation.

News of Luther's controversial stand was to cause a chain reaction across Europe, shaking both church and nations. The invention of the printing press some seventy years before meant that copies of Luther's 95 Theses rapidly spread across Europe. In sixteenth century Europe, nation states were rising up seeking their own identities and authority, and they too resented the power of the Pope and his bishops. It was said that Erasmus laid the egg that Luther hatched.

The news spread rapidly. Luther's archbishop reported 'this rash monk' to Rome. The Pope ordered that this monk's quarrel be quieted down. In 1518, Tetzel and the Dominicans accused Luther of heresy. Luther was an Augustinian and he had offended them. Luther explained his views on indulgences and grace in an open letter – in German, for all to read. He wrote, "*I know nothing about souls being dragged out of purgatory by an indulgence. I do not believe it...*" Luther visited Heidelberg to explain himself to fellow Augustinians and was well received, "*I went on foot and came back on a cart.*" The Dominicans continued to report Luther to Rome for heresy. As a result, Luther was ordered to appear before Cardinal Cajetan at Augsburg. It did not go well and friends smuggled Luther away to safety. "*I clearly saw my grave ready,*" he wrote in his journal. A change of emperors took attention away from Luther for a while but the new Holy Roman Emperor Charles V soon took up the challenge. In 1519, at the Leipzig Disputation, Luther entered a debate with theologian John Eck on the authority of Scripture and the church. Eck accused Luther of Hussite views, which had been condemned by the council. Luther said that Church Councils could be wrong. He was no longer just addressing the issue of indulgences. He was now challenging the authority of the Holy Mother Church of Rome itself.

By 1520, seeing that the papacy was not about to reform itself, Luther turned to writing Open Letters including one entitled, "Open Letter to the Christian Nobility of the German Nation concerning the Reform of the Christian Estate" followed by "Prelude on the Babylonish Captivity of the Church", and then another letter to the Pope called "The Freedom of the Christian Man," a writing that focuses on justification by faith alone. These are considered to be his three great 'Reformation Writings'. Luther argued that the church had taken the common people captive by controlling the sacraments. He attacked the withholding of the wine, the teaching of transubstantiation, the 'sacrifice' of the mass, absolution and penance. He accepted only two sacraments: baptism and the breaking of bread.

Luther was then excommunicated by the Pope and his books ordered to be burned, but many places, especially Wittenberg, would not publish the edict, or 'Papal Bull' as it was called. Erasmus, who had earlier been supportive, slowly drifted towards opposing Luther. Erasmus said at the time, '*The Church needs a Reformation: a Reformation viewed not as the work of one Pontiff nor of many cardinals, both of which the recent council demonstrated. It is the work of all Christendom. Better still, the work of God alone. Only He knows the hour of this reformation.*' Luther said, "*I await my excommunication from Rome any day now. On that account I have set all my affairs in order...*" Erasmus commented that Luther had, "*Hit the Pope on the crown and the monks in the belly.*"

In 1521, Luther was ordered to appear before the Emperor of the Holy Roman Empire at the Diet of Worms. Many pleaded with him not to go, fearing for his life. On arriving, he was asked to renounce his writings, but refused, asking for proof from Scripture that he was in error. *"Unless I am convinced by proofs from Scriptures or by plain and clear reasons and arguments, I can and I will not retract, for it is neither safe nor wise to do anything against conscience. Here I stand I can do no other!"* was his immortal response. On the journey home, he was 'kidnapped' and taken off to Wartburg Castle for his own safety and remained there for almost a year, in which time he translated much of the Bible into German.

Meanwhile, back in Wittenberg, the Reformation went on without Luther. His colleagues Carlstadt and Melanchthon had taken up the challenge. On Christmas Eve 1521, Philip Melanchthon celebrated the first evangelical Lord's Supper ever in the language of the German people.

1521 to 1525 was a period of embarrassing support for Luther and the Reformation. Peasants all over Germany saw these challenges as an opportunity to overthrow their masters. The ensuing Peasants' Revolt involved the destruction of bishops' palaces, monasteries and civic buildings. Knights, fearing for their authority, saw Luther as the saviour of Germany. With growing social and political unrest in Germany, accompanied with resentment against the power of Rome, Luther's 'rebellion' was attractive to many for mixed reasons. However, the peasants were brutally suppressed by the ruling classes with tens of thousand being slaughtered.

Philip of Hesse, a prince in Germany, supported Luther and sought to bring order and reformation to his domain. Others followed and the Catholic princes began to lose their influence. Luther was now able to work out his theology and address church practice. In 1525, he married a former nun, Katherine von Bora, who had been ejected from her convent by reformers. She had first come to Wittenberg seeking help from Luther. They had six children over the next few years. At the Diet of Speyer in 1526, the Catholics sought to enforce the Edict of Worms, but hostilities between the emperor and the Pope prevented this.

The Second Diet of Speyer, in 1529, was a setback, decreeing that the celebration of the mass should be imposed. Power was given to Catholic lords and princes to do so. It was here that the reformers lodged their 'Protest', giving rise to the name 'Protestants.'

The emperor called the Diet of Augsburg in 1530, to decide the fate of Luther and his followers. They were asked to present a confession of their position, the Confession of Augsburg. Written mainly by the conciliatory Melanchthon, even with his concessions, it was not acceptable to the Catholic theologians. The Confession of Augsburg was the first Protestant confession, greatly influencing later statements of faith such as the Thirty-Nine Articles of the Church of England. The threat of the Turks attacking at the edge of his lands forced the emperor to acquiesce with the Protestant princes and he called a recess. Essentially, this led to the formation of Protestant Princes in German whose lands and provinces became Lutheran.

Luther's view of God before his conversion was driven by terror of God and also a harsh domineering father who disapproved of his religious lifestyle. He struggled even after conversion to see God as a Father in a relational way. He admitted that calling God Father in the Lord's Prayer did not sit comfortably with him. But Luther was on a journey. He did not have all the truth that had been lost. His revelation was partial.

Luther undoubtedly rediscovered the forgotten truth of salvation by grace through faith in Jesus. His influence changed the course of the history of the church in the centuries to come. Like all, he had weaknesses and faults. He was often moody and depressed and given to very ungodly outbursts or orphan like behaviour. His attitude to Jews was dreadful and hard to justify on any grounds and was taken by future generations as support for anti Semitism. But he was a man of his time who God raised up to be the torch bearer of a move that would ultimately bring us fully home to Father.

Towards the end of his life, Luther often suffered with poor health and had bouts of depression, enduring considerable pain. He died at the end of 1546, aged 62 years.

THE SPREAD OF THE REFORMATION ACROSS EUROPE

The Catholic Princely states in Germany grouped together as the Catholic League and opposed the Protestant League in 1529 resulting in years of religious wars. But Lutheran ideas spread rapidly across Europe and into Scandinavia where the state church became Lutheran.

Reformation began in the independent Swiss Cantons when Ulrich Zwingli (1484 -1531) a Swiss reformer, influenced by Erasmus, began preaching. It is often said that Zwingli approached the reformation with his head as an intellectual, whereas Luther approached it with his heart, seeking personal peace with God. Zwingli laughed at indulgences while Luther wept. In some ways, he can be seen as a more thoroughgoing reformer than Luther, making a clean break with Rome. In 1519, he became a minister in Zurich, later preaching against indulgences and other Roman Catholic practices and proclaiming justification by faith. Zwingli differed with Luther over the Lord's Supper, taking a purely symbolic view of the bread and wine. All the northern Cantons of

Switzerland took up his views by 1529, where bishops were replaced with elders. He died in battle during a confrontation between hostile Cantons in 1531.

John Calvin (1509–1564) was perhaps the most prolific and influential theologian of the Protestant cause. Born in France to a privileged family and lifestyle, Calvin studied law at Paris and Orleans. In his early twenties, he became a Protestant, speaking of 'a sudden conversion'. He was a scholar and prolific writer, completing the first, slim edition of his *Institutes of the Christian Religion* in 1536 at the age of twenty-six, and wrote commentaries on almost every book of the Bible. Whilst travelling, he passed through Geneva where he intended to stay just one night, but he was to remain there for two years preaching, organising and directing church reforms. He then travelled to Strasbourg and Germany where he became a friend of Luther's colleague Philip Melanchthon. He returned to Geneva three years later to find division and antagonism between the churches and the civil authorities. The church in the city begged him to return and he did so, remaining twenty-three years until his death.

Calvin sought to build the churches of Geneva on Reformation theology. He had the full support of the city magistrates. He wielded enormous authority in the city, effecting 'church' discipline inside and outside the church. He achieved much for the city, introducing education for the young and care for the elderly. Inns and theatres were banned as Calvin sought to work his doctrine out into practice. Writing a generation after the first reformers, Calvin had less to do with controversy and more with clarification, formulating a systematic Reformed Theology.

Calvin's theology stemmed from a deep conviction concerning the transcendence and sovereignty of God. He was strongly in the tradition of Augustine. His weakness included hardness towards those who failed and lacked much sense of compassion, but he was not particularly different from any other religious or secular leaders of his age. They had rediscovered salvation through faith in Jesus Christ but knew little of the love of God as Father. That rediscovery was for others to find.

Reformation in France met resistance and persecution from King Francis I in 1545. However, there were 2000 centres of reformation across France by 1558. The terrible politically inspired massacre that took place on St. Bartholomew's Day 1572 in which 20,000 Protestants were slaughtered was the darkest night. Eventually, the Edict of Nantes in 1598 brought some degree of toleration for a while.

Calvinism in the Spanish Netherlands had to face the introduction of the Spanish Inquisition in 1555, which lead to terrible persecution and suffering for Protestants. When the Spanish were expelled, the Union of Utrecht in 1572 brought religious freedoms in Holland. The northern part of the Netherlands became predominantly reformed and Calvinist while the south remained Catholic.

Spain and Italy enthusiastically took up various aspects of reformation ideas but through the efforts of the Inquisition, all organized resistance was suppressed and destroyed. High in the Italian and French Alps, the Waldensian communities eagerly joined the Protestant cause in 1532.

As people began reading the Bible for themselves, they began to question infant baptism. A group in Zurich in 1522 began to baptize each other as believers. This brought the city council's wrath down on them within a few months. Zwingli spoke against them and in 1525, they were condemned to death by immersion in Lake Zurich. These people were called Anabaptists, meaning re-baptisers. Their ideas spread rapidly. Along with all other Protestants, they were condemned at the Diet of Speyer in 1529. They became a persecuted minority. One centre *where* were these radical reformers were in the majority was Munster in Germany where a wild element took over the city setting up a Kingdom of God on earth which among others things practiced polygamy. It ended in 1534 when the city was attacked and all the Anabaptists executed. Both Reformers and Catholics persecuted them. As a result they fled to the fringes of Europe to the watery wastes of Holland, to Moravia and Poland. Here they remained and merged with Hussites and formed an alternative radical expression of Christianity. In the next century, they were known as Hutterites settling in Bohemia and Slovakia and passed on their spiritual heritage to the Moravians.

Menno Simons (1496 – 1561) was the main thinker of the Anabaptist movement and led the scattered communities in Holland. Religious toleration gave them a strong base in the low countries especially Amsterdam. The Mennonites eventually emigrated in large numbers to America *where* were they still live today in isolated rural communities and are also known as Amish and Pennsylvania Dutch.

THE MAIN TENETS OF REFORMATION THEOLOGY

It is important to pause at this point and look at what the basic beliefs of Reformation theology were. They fall into these main areas: justification by faith, the authority of Scripture with tradition alongside the Scriptures, a rethinking of the sacraments and the doctrine of the Church and predestination. Many of these beliefs had been lost for many centuries. However, some were new and because of that needed to be looked at. Many in the new reformed churches taught them but this was not universal. A number were even adopted by later Catholic thinkers.

Justification by faith alone lies at the heart of the Reformation, leading the Reformers into conflict with the Roman Catholic Church over the practice of selling indulgences and the power the church exercised over the people through the sacraments.

"God does not want to save us by our own personal and private righteousness and wisdom. He wants to save us by a righteousness and wisdom apart from, and other than this: a righteousness that does not come from ourselves and is not brought to birth by ourselves. It is a righteousness that comes into us from somewhere else. It is not a righteousness that finds its origin on earth. It is a righteousness which comes from heaven." So wrote Luther in 1515 when lecturing on the book of Romans. *Jesus, more specifically!*

The Reformers argued their case on the authority of Scripture. The Catholic Church maintained that it was the Pope's prerogative to interpret Scripture and only his interpretation was valid and authoritative. A clash of views was inevitable as these were the days of the Renaissance when the Scriptures were being rediscovered and translated from original manuscripts. *'The Bible is the religion of the Protestants'* was one slogan; *'by Scripture alone'* was another. The authority of the Church, Popes, and Councils was now held to be subordinate to Scripture. The Bible used throughout the Middle Ages had been the Vulgate, a translation into Latin by Jerome in the early fifth century. Wycliffe's translation of the Bible into English was a translation of the Vulgate. New versions in the various languages of Europe under the influence of Erasmus and the Humanists began to be produced. An attempt was made to go back to the original languages. This led to several changes from the Vulgate and brought vitality to the Scriptures, particularly the experience of the risen Christ in the New Testament. Erasmus held that to give the laity the Bible in their own language was the key to renewal.

The decision was made by Luther to reject the books known as the Apocrypha from having canonical status. One implication was that teaching such as 'prayers for the dead' was rejected.

There was, however, one compromise. The Reformers accepted the authority not just of Scripture, but Scripture and its interpretation by the Church Fathers, where such interpretation could be justified. As a result, they maintained belief in the Trinity, the Divinity of Christ and infant baptism. The Anabaptists however, rejected tradition and based authority solely on Scripture, "Sola scriptura".

By the end of the Middle Ages, the Roman Catholic Church recognised seven sacraments, taken as physical signs signifying the grace of God or the gracious action of God. They were: Baptism, Eucharist, Penance, Confirmation, Marriage, Ordination, and Extreme Unction. The Protestant Reformers accepted only two of these, baptism and Eucharist. Luther strongly attacked the Catholic view of the Eucharist, known as 'transubstantiation' which is the belief that the bread and wine actually changed into the body and blood of Christ leaving no bread and wine present. Luther asserted that Christ is really present and called this 'consubstantiation', or the Real Presence. Zwingli argued, however, that since Christ is seated at the right hand of God, wherever this might be, his body is not present in the Eucharist. Whereas Luther claimed that the expression, 'this is my body' meant exactly what it said. Zwingli gave it the meaning, 'this represents my body', with the communion as a visible demonstration of faith.

As far as baptism was concerned the Reformers accepted the idea of infant baptism. The arguments they used to support it was that it covered original sin and that it was a sign of God's free grace, inspiring faith at a later time. They taught that it was the New Covenant equivalent of circumcision in the Old Covenant to be administered in infancy. They acknowledged that many infants died young and felt they needed to be baptised as early as possible. Anabaptists taught that infant baptism was invalid in that it required no faith by the infant. Instead, they began to see baptism as a sign following repentance and justification by faith for believers.

The Reformers believed that the church was the company of people who heard the Word, including those predestined by God who had not yet come to faith, so you could never be totally sure who the true believers were. The Reformers therefore believed that the preaching of the Word was the church's highest calling and not the administration of the sacraments. The Anabaptists, however, felt that a local church was a company of true believers only.

Calvin defined the true church as being one in which the word of God was preached and the sacraments rightly administered. The Catholic Church did not qualify on these grounds, he asserted, so you were justified in leaving the Catholic Church. His concept of the church was an ordered, disciplined structure on New Testament lines, with the offices of minister, elder and deacon. He envisaged the church as the visible community of believers, together with the invisible fellowship of the saints and company of the elect. The visible form would include both the elect and reprobate, as in the parable of the wheat and tares growing together. *"Wherever we see the Word of God purely preached and listened to, and the sacraments administered according to the institution of Christ, we must not doubt that there is the church"* (Calvin).

The Reformers viewed the world as God's world in contrast to the monastic views of Catholicism that regarded the world as hopeless and a place to withdraw from. The Reformation asserted the glory of God's creation and redemption of the world. The Reformers valued work as a vocation, as service to the Creator, as enjoying the development of the natural world. This is described as the Protestant work ethic. The Reformers taught in accordance with Scripture that rulers must be supported and obeyed to help them perform their God-given duties of government. But equally, if rulers exceed what is justly given to them by God, then they may no longer be considered as rulers, and may be justly opposed. *"God pays no attention to the significance of the work being done, but looks at the heart which is serving Him in the work. This is true even of such everyday tasks as washing dishes or milking cows"* (Luther).

The Reformers taught that the complement to the faith of the believer is the grace of God. The freedom of the individual to choose or choose not to believe in God raised the question of the sovereignty of God. Zwingli was in no doubt that the sovereignty of God is paramount. Augustine had been content to see, for the justified ones, God's grace happily matching the human decision. But what about those who did not respond? His reply was that God passes them over. For Calvin, the logic made it impossible to accept that God chooses some and simply ignores the others. Predestination for Calvin meant that God actively chooses to redeem or condemn each individual. While Luther could state that God saves sinners despite their demerits, Calvin asserted that God saves individuals irrespective of their merits.

From 1570, the doctrine of the 'Elect' became dominant in Reformed

Theology. Through this teaching, the Reformed believers could identify themselves with Israel in the sense of being God's elect people, and this doctrine of election was the inspiration of the Puritans. It left the huge issue of the rest, those who were not predestined for salvation by the sovereign God. Future generations of hyper Calvinists would comfortably teach that God predestines some for salvation and the rest for damnation. This is the dead end that began with Tertullian was watered by Augustine and replanted by Calvin.

CHAPTER NINE

Reformation in England and Beyond

HENRY VIII AND THE CHURCH OF ENGLAND

1500's

English history of the early sixteenth century is dominated by the giant figure of King Henry VIII. His most prominent act, with repercussions for today and beyond, was his break with the Roman Catholic Church. Relations with Rome were already uneasy, as typified by the attempted reforms of Wycliffe and the Lollards. Henry's dispute with the Pope was over his need for a divorce from Catherine of Aragon. It was the 'king's great matter' that was the occasion for the split and not the direct cause. Henry VIII was a sincere Catholic and had written a tract against Luther in which he said, "I assert there are seven sacraments," for which the Pope in gratitude gave him the title 'Defender of the Faith' which is still held by the British monarch.

Henry's marriage to Catherine had produced numerous pregnancies but only one child, a daughter, Mary. He wanted a son and he wanted to divorce Catherine. The Pope refused permission and so Henry, who felt he could rely on the support of the English people, chose to declare his independence from Rome. He established an independent Church of England governed by him. In 1532, he appointed the reformer Thomas Cranmer as the Archbishop of Canterbury. Cranmer granted the divorce and five days later Henry married his mistress Anne Boleyn.

Henry's second marriage produced another daughter, Elizabeth, but Anne fell from favour and was beheaded. Jane Seymour, Henry's third wife died shortly after giving birth to his only son and heir, Edward. Henry was not a supporter of Luther, with whom he clashed a number of times, and his desire was to follow the doctrines of the Catholic Church, but without allegiance to the Pope.

As a result, Henry was the ruler of all matters in both state and church in England. While opposing the concept of Protestantism, he was happy to use Luther's scorn on the abuses of Rome as justification for his actions. In 1531, Henry gave himself the title, 'Supreme Head of the Church and of the Clergy', but to demonstrate his standing as a good Catholic, ordered the destruction of the works of Wycliffe, Luther and Zwingli. Conversely, Henry appointed Thomas Cromwell known as the 'monk-mauler' to appropriate all monastic property in England. This was known as the dissolution of the monasteries.

WILLIAM TYNDALE
- REDISCOVERS GOD'S FATHERHEART

William Tyndale (1494–1536) lived through the years of Henry's reign and is best known for his translation of the New Testament. Whereas Wycliffe had translated the Bible into English from the Latin Vulgate over a hundred years earlier, Tyndale was able to translate from the more accurate Greek manuscripts. Although Henry had thrown off the rule of the Pope in his realm, England was still a dangerous place for reformers and Lutheran ideas. Consequently, Tyndale was forced to flee to Europe to translate the Scriptures. His translation of the New Testament was published in 1525 and had widespread influence, a large part of it passing directly into the King James' Version. Tyndale said of this achievement to a cleric who criticised him, "...*if God spare my life, ere many years pass, I will cause a boy that driveth the plough shall know more of the Scriptures than thou dost.*"

A closer examination of Tyndale's work reveals some amazing surprises. Generally, the Reformers thought of God the Father as someone who was remote from us. However, as Ralph Werrell says, "*When we turn to William Tyndale we find we enter a new theological world — a world which leaves behind that the Father is in heaven and we are on earth with a great gap between us; into a world of a true, living, personal relationship between God the Father and his child*" (Ralph S. Werrell, *The Theology of William Tyndale*. Cambridge: James Clarke & Co. Ltd., 2006).

Love is the key to Tyndale's theology of the Fatherhood of God, and of the Christian being a son of God.

> "*The love of God to us-ward is exceeding great, in that he hath made us his sons, without all deserving of us; and hath given us his Spirit through Christ, to certify our hearts thereof, in that we feel that our trust is in God, and that our souls have received health and power to love the law of God; which is a sure testimony that we are sons, and under no damnation.*"
>
> - TYNDALE, *EXPOSITION 1 JOHN*, PS2, P. 186.

Tyndale frequently stresses that God's love for man goes back to the creation, a fact that takes away any idea that our salvation has anything to do with our reception of the gospel; whether by faith, our good works, or by anything that God sees in us. The first thing he emphasizes about the relationship between God the Father and his children is the warmth, the tenderness and the love he shows to them.

"As affirmeth Paul saying: which loved us in his beloved before the creation of the world. For the love that God hath to Christ / he loveth us / and not for our own sakes"

- TYNDALE, *1525, PROLOGE*, P. 4.

Tyndale expands this in his *Answer.*

"God is ever fatherly-minded toward the elect members of his church. He loved them, before the world began, in Christ (Eph. 1). He loveth them while they be yet evil, and his enemies in their hearts, ere they be come unto the knowledge of his Son Christ, and ere his law be written in their hearts; as a father loveth his young son, while he is yet evil, and ere it know the father's law to consent thereto."

- TYNDALE, *ANSWER*, PS3, P.IIIF.

And we experience the work of the Father in our lives as we become alive to him and his will for us.

"In Christ God chose us, and elected us before the beginning of the world, created us anew by the word of the gospel, and put his Spirit in us, for because that we should do good works. A Christian man worketh, because it is the will of his Father only."

- TYNDALE, *MAMMON, PS1, P.77.*

In William Tyndale, we have a man way ahead of all the other reformers in his understanding of the love of God the Father and our position in Christ as sons. Sadly, Tyndale's teachings and deep understanding of these truths have been largely forgotten but are worthy of thought and study. In 1535, ten years after the publication of his New Testament, Tyndale was betrayed, strangled, and burnt at the stake in Brussels, before he was able to complete his translation of the Old Testament.

ENGLISH REFORMATION AND CATHOLIC RESURGENCE

Thomas Cranmer (1489 – 1556), Henry's Archbishop of Canterbury was a committed Lutheran and a genuinely godly man. He worked through a remarkable and difficult relationship with Henry to bring a proper spiritual dimension to the new Church of England. He produced, with Henry's approval, the Ten Articles of 1536 *"to establish Christian quietness and unity in the land and to avoid contentious opinions."* This was followed by the stronger set of Injunctions that required clergy to teach the Creed, the Lord's Prayer and the Ten Commandments, with a Bible to be placed in every parish church in Latin, but eventually in English. Tyndale's translation of the Bible was politically unacceptable, so Cranmer commissioned Miles Coverdale to produce a version that became available and began to be used in churches in 1539. Henry called Cranmer to his deathbed in 1547, and decreed that his succession should be in the order: Edward, Mary, and then Elizabeth.

Cranmer began his major work of compiling the Book of Common Prayer. His first version demonstrated his loyalty to Henry in a prayer, subsequently deleted, *'from the tyranny of the Bishop of Rome and all his detestable enormities, good Lord deliver us'*. Cranmer's wording to receive the bread remained as *"The body of our Lord Jesus Christ which was given for you... Take and eat this in remembrance that Christ died for you, and feed on Him in your heart by faith with thanksgiving."*

Edward VI (1537 – 1553) came to the throne at the age of nine. In a typically English compromise, Henry had ensured that his son be tutored by protestant reformers. Edward was perceived as a godly, spiritual and scholarly king albeit just a boy who with Cranmer enabled the spiritual change in England to gain momentum. He reigned just six years.

Yet in those six years, the contrast with his father could hardly be greater. In his Act of Uniformity of 1549, he legalised the first Book of Prayer with simplified services to be held in English based on Scripture.

Cranmer desired for the Church of England, a church that had a theology and spirituality continuous with the church founded by Jesus Christ. He wrote the 39 Articles of Faith for the new church, defining its totally evangelical doctrines, while opposing both the Roman Catholics and Anabaptists. He followed Luther on Faith and Justification, and concerning the sacraments, he believed in the Real Presence, except that Christ was present through the faith of the believer. Edward VI died at age fifteen after a life of much sickness. As Edward drew near to death, there was great concern about the succession of Mary, a fanatical Catholic and the effect she would have on the nation. The Earl of Northumberland urged Edward to change the succession, and concede the crown to his daughter-in-law, Lady Jane Grey, a young, accomplished and godly lady, the great granddaughter of Henry VII. There was, however, little appetite for this intrigue from the other nobles who largely welcomed Mary. Mary began her reign by having this innocent and naïve young couple executed.

" Bloody "

Mary I became Queen of England in 1553. She was the bastardized daughter of Catherine of Aragon, an intolerant Catholic and a sad tragic girl rejected by her father, determined to reverse the Reformation, restore Roman Catholicism and re-establish the authority of the Pope in England. She sought an alliance through her marriage to the Catholic, Philip of Spain. She immediately repealed the legislation of Edward VI, dismissed the Protestant bishops, and brought back Cardinal Pole, exiled in Henry's time, as her Archbishop. The leading evangelical bishops, Nicholas Ridley and Hugh Latimer were imprisoned and burnt at the stake in Oxford on 16 October 1555. As the flames licked around them at the stake, Latimer famously said, *"Be of good comfort, Master Ridley, and play the man; we shall this day light such a candle by God's grace in England, as I trust will never be put out."* The aged Bishop Hooper of Gloucester was burned before the silent and weeping people of the city. Clergy were sacked and many fled abroad. Hundreds of laity, including whole families, were attacked, imprisoned and burned.

Cranmer was given a long process of interrogation and mental torture in prison, including being forced to watch the Oxford burnings of Ridley and Latimer. Eventually, he was worn down and confused enough to sign a recantation. A 'show' execution was arranged in which the climax would be Cranmer's declaration of his conversion to Rome. Instead, Cranmer first thrust into the flames the hand that had signed the recantation, then declared his renunciation of this confession, and declared his faith in Christ. *"As for the Pope, I refuse him, as Christ's enemy and antichrist, and all his false doctrine."* Cranmer, therefore, died at the stake on 21 March 1556. Mary ordered at least three hundred more executions. She died bitter, childless, unloved by her husband and detested as 'bloody Mary' by most of the English. Cardinal Pole died twelve hours later.

A TALE OF TWO QUEENS IN ENGLAND AND SCOTLAND

Elizabeth I (1532 – 1603) had an unusual childhood. At the age of three, her father, the King, beheaded her mother. Her only brother died young. Her only sister Mary had her imprisoned in the Tower with threats to kill her unless she changed her religion. Yet, she became one of the greatest monarchs in British history. She came to the throne at a politically precarious and crucial time. Ravaged by civil war, Catholics persecuted Huguenots in France, and the Counter-Reformation was revitalising the Catholic Church. The new Jesuit order was winning converts around the world, and the Inquisition was enforcing Catholic doctrine, particularly in Spain and Italy. Protestant refugees from the continent brought with them their beliefs, in many cases based on Calvin's teachings, desiring to see reform along the lines of Calvin's Geneva.

Although anti-papal, Elizabeth took a conservative line. She chose a policy of national unity and resumed the cautious church reforms started by Henry and Edward. Within months of coming to the throne, she passed the Acts of Supremacy and Uniformity. These acts had the effect of making Elizabeth Supreme Governor of the Church in England in the realm of all causes spiritual and temporal as her father Henry had been.

She repealed the Acts of Mary and re-authorised a new Prayer Book. Every person was required to attend Sunday service in the Church of England with a fine of a shilling for non-attendance. There were injunctions to the clergy to teach, preach, read the Bible, make pastoral visits, care for the poor, keep parish registers, and properly observe Sundays.

The Pope excommunicated Elizabeth in 1570, releasing English Catholics from allegiance to the Queen. Their rallying point was Mary,

Queen of Scots, Elizabeth's cousin, and a prisoner in England. The Catholics perceived Mary as a claimant for the English crown. Faced with these powerful threats, Elizabeth had Mary arrested tried and executed for treason. The justification was the over-riding need for national unity and security in the face of the surrounding threats.

In the early sixteenth century, Scotland was backward spiritually and open to all the worst excesses of medieval religion. Gradually, as news of the Lutheran Reformation came to the country, Scottish reformers began to preach against sin and called for faith and salvation. This aroused such fierce opposition that an act was passed in 1535 to ban heretical books, and many were martyred for their faith. One of the leading preachers, George Wishart, returned in 1543 to continue his ministry, but he was burnt at the stake in 1546. He was strongly defended by his friend, John Knox (1510 – 1572) who escaped and came to England in 1549, working with Cranmer on the Second Book of Common Prayer, in 1552. On his return to Scotland, Knox led a covenant with other Scottish Protestants, forming the 'Congregation of Jesus Christ'.

Mary, Queen of Scots, who had come to the throne at the age of six days, then ruled the country. Henry VIII had hoped she would be married to Edward, uniting the two countries, but Edward's premature death prevented this, and Mary, an ardent Catholic, married instead, King Francis of France. Francis died after only a year of marriage, but the association with France enabled Mary to call on French troops for military support in attempting to repress the Scottish Reformation. Knox was so affronted by the presence of two Catholic queens that he wrote his hysterical polemic, 'First blast of the Trumpet against the Monstrous Regiment of Women' in 1558.

The Scottish Covenanters led by Knox gained increasing support from the people, and their faith and determination enabled them to stand firm against the Queen and her French troops. The increasing desire for political union between England and Scotland was reinforced by the wishes of Protestants in both countries, for a single Protestant kingdom. The growing bond was greatly strengthened by the English troops under Elizabeth I, who drove the French out of Scotland in 1560. This solidarity among the English and Scottish nobility was a major factor in the political establishment of Protestantism in Britain.

Mary, Queen of Scots, was deposed and replaced as monarch by her infant son, James VI, in 1567. She took refuge in England and remained virtually under house arrest for the next twenty years, before being executed for an alleged association in a plot to seize the English crown. Ironically, her son, James VI of Scotland, became James I of England in 1603. The only distinguishing feature of his uninspired reign was the publication of the Authorised Version of the Bible in 1611, which is referred to as the King James Version. One significant fact was that the translators of the King James Bible used William Tyndale's translation of the Bible extensively.

Moynahan writing about the King James Version says, "A complete analysis of the Authorised Version, known down the generations as "the AV" or "the King James Version" was made in 1998. It shows that Tyndale's words account for 84% of the New Testament and for 75.8% of the Old Testament books that he translated." Joan Bridgman makes the comment in the *Contemporary Review* that, "He [Tyndale] is the mainly unrecognised translator of the most influential book in the world" (Bridgman, Joan (2000), "Tyndale's New Testament", *Contemporary Review* 277 (1619): 342–46).

Ireland had Anglicanism imposed on it by Henry VIII and his protestant successors. Large numbers of Scottish Presbyterians were settled in Ulster during the reign of Elizabeth I that were to cause problems in later centuries.

ROMAN CATHOLIC COUNTER REFORMATION

The Catholic Church did not just sit back and let the reformers take all the initiatives. The Popes fought back with every weapon at their disposal. The time-honoured method of dealing with issues was to call a Church Council. This was duly convened in 1545 in the city of Trento in northern Italy. The Council of Trent gathered on and off for over 18 years from 1545 to 1563 in an attempt to respond to the Protestant challenges. The outcome was that Catholicism was restated and defined and the seven sacraments reaffirmed. Purgatory and indulgences that had been taught for centuries were defined along with both faith and works being necessary for salvation. The Mass and papal authority were confirmed. A list of prohibited books known as the Index was drawn up which included the Bible in any language other than Latin and the Vulgate was the only approved version. It insisted on the Apocrypha being retained, and forbade anyone to publish any interpretation of Scripture, unless authorized by church superiors. A series of anathemas or curses were pronounced on all who believed or taught anything different to approved Catholic doctrine.

The Inquisition was employed widely in lands where Catholic monarchs ruled. In France, in 1545, four thousand Waldensians were executed. In the Spanish Netherlands, 100,000 Anabaptists, Mennonites and Protestants were killed. In Spain, Protestants were wiped out and in 1572, 22,000 French Huguenots were massacred. They also targeted Jews and Muslims throughout Europe.

New religious orders were formed. The most famous was the Jesuits. This new order, known as the Society of Jesus, was founded in 1534 by Ignatius Loyola, a Spanish noble(1491 – 1556). In 1523, he spent a year in a monastery at Montserrat praying and meditating. As a result, he wrote a work called *The Spiritual Exercises*. This became the basis of the Society of Jesus. One of his closest followers was Francis Xavier (1502 – 1552) who, as a Jesuit Missionary, took Catholicism to the east. Xavier established missionary bases in India, Goa, China and Japan. As Spain and Portugal opened up the New World, Jesuits went with them. All their colonies in Central and South America had Catholic Missions as part of their colonization and indigenous peoples were "encouraged" to convert to Roman Catholicism.

In Europe, the Jesuits became ardent inquisitors and activists in bringing people back to the 'true' faith. They founded a college in Douay in Belgium specifically to train English Catholics to infiltrate and overthrow Elizabethan England. Many entered the country covertly and were protected by some of the aristocracy. It was the age of priest holes, the secret chambers built into the homes of Catholic nobles to hide the priests. Most were caught and executed. They were the force behind such plots as the attempt by Guy Fawkes to blow up the English parliament and king. Their most notorious value was that they believed the end justified the means. By 1626, there were over four hundred Jesuit colleges with 15,544 Jesuit priests.

Catholics, whilst getting a lot of bad press from Protestants, had many examples of people very open to what God was doing. There were countless genuine believers within Catholicism. In particular, Catholic mysticism flourished as they tried to revitalize their faith. Teresa of Avila (1515 – 1582), a Spanish Carmelite nun, became a leading figure in the mystical and contemplative approach. She was highly disciplined and often described ecstatic experiences and visions of Jesus. John of the Cross (1542 – 1591) preached all over Spain calling people to a simple faith in Jesus and unbroken fellowship with God. He experienced a number of miraculous healings in his ministry. He said, *"If we are guided by divine Scripture we shall not be able to err, for he who speaks in it is the Holy Spirit."* Nonetheless, in his lifetime, he was persecuted by many of the Roman Catholic clergy and his writings viewed with great suspicion. Yet, 150 years after his death, Benedict XIII accorded him the title of saint.

CHAPTER TEN

Revival

Every move of God or new wave of reformation and revival seems to have lasted about one generation or two generations at most. Each new generation needs to have its own experience of God moving and not rely on the move of God in a previous generation. The history of the church over the next four hundred years bares this out. Within a very short time, the second or third generation sets the last move of God into stone, becoming legalistic and cold. Sadly, they also typically become the persecutors of the next move of God. At the same time, there is always a godly desire in some to move on into what God has for their generation and an unwillingness to settle. The church of the next few centuries was a mix of settlers who wanted to preserve the past and pioneers who wanted to press into the next things God had. The result was often conflict, misunderstanding and division along with the desire to keep in step with what God was doing.

PURITANS, PILGRIM FATHERS AND PIETISTS

1600's

At the beginning of the seventeenth century, there was frustration at the perceived compromises of church reformation in England under Elizabeth. The struggle between the 'old' and 'new' lasted longer than in Europe. Despite many changes, the church remained unsatisfactory both to Catholics, and the more extreme Protestants. Many wanted a clearer break with Roman ways, and a more thoroughgoing reformation based on Calvinistic teaching. Those who held these views were known as Puritans because they wished to purify the church from its popish traditions. These Puritans who were still members of the Church of England, wanted to see a fully reformed church. They wanted to see something more along the lines of Calvin's Geneva. The Puritans had strong support in Parliament and held very high hopes of achieving their reforms. They opposed the wearing of clerical vestments, viewing them as 'rags of popery'. They were against traditions such as the signing of the cross and kneeling at communion as it could be confused with the adoration of the elements and observing of saints' days.

They strongly encouraged competent, biblical preaching, household prayers, Bible study and godly lifestyle. They were strongly Trinitarian and believed in one single catholic - meaning universal - church. The scriptures alone were seen as the basis and norm for all doctrine. They practiced baptism and observed the Lord's Supper. Worship was always in the mother tongue and centred on Christ. They saw all men as sinners saved only through forgiveness offered by God in Christ, justification by faith alone and that all the justified would rise again at the Last Day.

As official opposition grew towards the Puritans and other dissenting groups, many went abroad to Amsterdam and to Ulster to seek freedom of religion. John Milton, who wrote *Paradise Lost* at this time, was a Puritan.

Change, however, did not come easily. King James I of the newly unified Kingdom of England and Scotland, who reigned from 1603–1625, was as adamant as Elizabeth I had been against the Puritans, with his 'High Church' sympathies. High Church began to be recognized as meaning theoretically Protestant yet with practices that were typically from the Roman Catholic tradition. Opposition grew, and small groups grew up alongside the Puritans. These 'Separatists' (or 'Dissenters'), led by Robert Browne and Robert Harrison, felt they could no longer regard the Church of England as a true church and in 1581 they left. With their followers, they formed an independent congregation in Norwich. This marked the beginning of the Independents in England later known as Congregationalists. Harassment and repression followed and many fled abroad to Holland and Ireland. Many others were imprisoned. John Smythe, a Separatist and a former fellow of Christ's College, was baptized in Amsterdam in 1608. Thomas Helwys, an earlier associate of John Smythe in Amsterdam, returned to England after Smythe's death and formed the first English Baptist congregation in London in 1612. James I response was *"I will make them conform themselves or I will harry them out of the land, or else do worse."* However, by 1625, there were many dissenting groups meeting in England.

An early group of dissenters led by John Robinson sought refuge in Holland. In 1620, they left Leiden in Holland and sailed via Plymouth to America seeking the peace and religious freedom denied them in England. Robinson said in 1620, *"The Lord has more truth yet to break forth from his word."* By 1640, 20,000 pilgrims had left the shores of England and founded the many new settlements that made up New England on the North American coast. The colonists faced a lengthy series of challenges, from bureaucracy, impatient investors and internal conflicts to sabotage, storms, disease, and uncertain relations with the First Nations of North America. The colony, established in 1620, became the second successful English settlement in what was to become the United States of America. The first was Jamestown, Virginia, founded in 1607. Their story has become a central theme of the history and culture of the United States.

Matters worsened considerably under James' son, Charles I in the United Kingdom. He was very much a 'High Church' man and in 1633 appointed William Laud as Archbishop of Canterbury. The church took up many 'catholic' practices again. Those who resisted were punished severely. Charles' catholic marriage and ill-fated dealings with Scotland led to opposition from Parliament and the Scots. Civil War broke out in 1642 in which Oliver Cromwell (1599 – 1658) played a prominent part in the struggle against Charles I. English Parliamentarians and Puritans, aided by the Scots, went to war against Charles and his Royalists supporters.

The victory of Parliament and the imposition of the Commonwealth on England ensured Archbishop Laud's execution and eventually King Charles himself was also beheaded. The Puritans demanded radical change with strong support from the Scottish Presbyterians. The Westminster Assembly, which met in 1646, was made up primarily of Puritans from England and Scotland. They produced the Westminster Confession of 1647 that distilled Puritan thought and had a strong influence on Western Protestantism. One of its most famous statements is, *"What is the chief end of man? A man's chief end is to glorify God and enjoy him forever."* The defeat of Charles I by Cromwell saw a flourishing of dissent and freedom to explore new forms of worship.

In this period of toleration and religious freedom, all manner of groups emerged and flourished for a short while. Some were serious and godly. Others were odd, such as the Adamites who believed that worship should be conducted like Adam before the fall - that is naked. It attracted a lot of enthusiastic naturists. A bizarre group known as Muggletonians appeared at this time. They believed that anyone who rejected their teachings would go to hell. To spare them this fate they forbade their followers from telling anyone what they believed thus effectively banning evangelism. The last Muggletonian died in 1940.

[handwritten margin note: Quakers' history / Penn sylvania = Penn's forest]

Another group led by George Fox (1624 – 1691) called The Religious Society of Friends emerged at this time. He was weary of formal religion, with the English Church always under state control offering protection rather than spirituality. After his conversion at age twenty-two, he began an itinerant preaching ministry that lasted forty years. He traveled all over England, Scotland and Ireland, Holland and to America. God's presence often fell in his meeting as he prayed, *they* ~~there~~ were speaking in tongues at times as they sat and waited on the presence of God. He and his followers were given the derisive name Quakers, due to their 'trembling' in meetings under the presence of the power of God. By 1660, there were over 50,000 Quakers with a colony started by William Penn (1644 – 1718) in America called Pennsylvania. Sadly, the long cherished religious liberty did not last.

In 1660, the monarchy was restored. Charles II came back from France to England bringing with him strong Catholic leanings. Repression quickly followed with the Act of Uniformity demanding total acceptance of the Anglican Prayer book by all. Laws repressing non-conforming ministers caused many to resign their livings and many were imprisoned. John Bunyan (1628 -1688) was imprisoned over a period of twelve years in Bedford prison, where he wrote *The Pilgrim's Progress*, which became one of the most influential books of the age.

The Scottish Church had bishops forced on it and many resisters, known as Covenanters, were executed. Once again, people fled abroad. Many Quakers went to America with William Penn. By 1690, there were some 250,000 British dissenters in North America. Extreme persecution under the infamous Judge Jeffery caused even the bishops to revolt.

James II fled to France and was replaced by his daughter Mary and her Dutch Protestant husband William of Orange who introduced the 'Toleration Act' of 1689. However, this proved to be a mixed blessing. 'Toleration' included a much wider range of theological views and all groups suffered a decline in religious vitality. Extremism of any form was feared and moderation ruled. Denominations were now tolerated, but in all the churches there was little passion or conviction.

In mainland Europe, there was great religious turmoil. Jacobus Arminius (1560 – 1609) was a Dutch pastor and theologian who had been taught by Theodore Beza, Calvin's handpicked successor. He rejected his teacher's theology that it is God who unconditionally elects some for salvation. Instead, Arminius proposed that the election of God was *of believers*, thereby making it conditional on faith. The Dutch Calvinists challenged Arminius' views, but Arminius died before a national synod could occur.

Arminianism holds to the following beliefs: humans are naturally unable to make any effort towards salvation since salvation is possible by grace alone. Works of human effort cannot cause or contribute to salvation. God's election is conditional on faith in Jesus. Jesus' atonement was for all people. God allows his grace to be resisted by those unwilling to believe and salvation can be lost, as continued salvation is conditional upon continued faith. John Wesley, founder of the Methodist movement, embraced Arminian theology and became its most prominent champion. Today, Methodism remains committed to Arminian theology, and Arminianism itself has become one of the dominant theological systems in the United States.

For Europe, the third phase of Catholic Counter Reformation started in 1618 as an attempt to force Roman Catholic control on areas of Europe that had turned to Protestantism. It resulted in the Thirty Years War. For Germany, it was an unmitigated evil. For a generation, the land was plundered from end to end. The population fell from 16 million to 6 million. The cycle of war and religious conflict left people weary. The old religious struggles had now become political and the seeds of decay, morally and spiritually, were sown.

This dismal state of affairs was addressed in Europe by the rise of the 'Pietists'. They grew out of the Dutch Reformed Church in the early seventeenth century. They were brought to fruition in the Lutheran Church. Early Pietists like Philip Spener (1635 – 1705) wanted to see reformed lives within a reformed church. Spener set up house-meetings for prayer, Bible study and the sharing of Christian experience. This was not without its critics, who accused them of being legalistic, and misunderstood their desire to reform within the church.

In France, Protestants who were known as the Huguenots were continually persecuted and over 400,000 eventually fled to England, the Netherlands and one group went to the new Colony at the Cape of Good Hope to seek freedom to practice their faith.

INDIFFERENCE AND TOLERANCE IN THE 18TH CENTURY

George I in England was indifferent to Christianity and many people's personal faith collapsed. God was seen as a distant inflexible taskmaster. All that had gone before seemed to count for little. Drunkenness, lax morals and little evidence of spiritual vitality was prominent. The picture was bleak. Whilst there was a new mood of tolerance towards religion, this was more to do with weariness and indifference than understanding.

Three philosophical ideas that developed at this time gripped the minds of people. The first was Rationalism. This was the belief that human reason, not God's revelation was the final arbiter in all affairs. Then came Empiricism, which taught that only what can be seen, touched and heard was real thus ruling out all ideas of faith or the supernatural. Many Christians adopted Deism, the view that God existed but had lost interest in humanity and was distant, abstract and unknowable. Religion became cold and formal. The Bible began to be attacked critically and Christ deity denied. Crime increased, social unrest grew, moral standards collapsed and drunkenness became a scourge of the common people. In France, the decline culminated in the French Revolution during which a goddess of reason was enthroned in Notre Dame in 1789. The revolutionaries sought to banish the church and the monarchy from French life altogether, ending the 'divine right' of monarchs. Alongside these events, new intellectual thinkers such as Voltaire in France and Thomas Jefferson in America, brought in a radical intellectualism in a period called 'the Enlightenment'. Philosophers like Voltaire attacked, by virtue of human reason, the consequences as well as the content of the Reformation and its aftermath. It was a very dark day for the Church and Christianity.

C. Baxter Krueger sums up the Enlightenment like this, *"Between 1600 and 1800, Western Christianity suffered two direct and brutal hits, which devastated its mind and heart, shattered its confidence, and left the Church utterly floundering in the throes of irrelevance. In the period known as the Enlightenment (also known as The Age of Reason), the completion of a massive shift took place in the way the Western mind thinks about God, about the universe, and about human existence and its nature, purpose and destiny. Such a shift was 1000 years in the making, and has its roots in the great St. Augustine himself (354 - 430). The Enlightenment is indeed*

Augustine's stepchild, born of Augustine's unholy marriage of Greek philosophy and Christian revelation. It was a long time in coming, but Augustine's stepchild finally came of age and broke free from the shackles of Christian authority. Unconverted human reason (or to be more blunt, pagan thinking) rose with such considerable force that the Christian vision of the universe was overthrown and a radically secular worldview took its place" (*Recovering the Trinity and Perichoresis and Their Significance For the 3rd Christian Millennium*, Perichoresis Lectures 2002, Adelaide Australia).

ZINZENDORF AND THE MORAVIANS

As in all ages, amid the decline and darkness there were signs of true spirituality and faith. In the midst of the darkness and decline in Europe, there was a stirring. Philip Spener's godson Nikolaus Ludwig, Count von Zinzendorf, was influenced by German Pietism. Born into Austrian nobility and raised by his grandmother, Zinzendorf showed an early inclination toward theology and religious work. As the godson of Spener, he was raised in a strong Pietist tradition.

In Bohemia, there were Christians known as Moravians who were the spiritual descendants of the fifteenth century reformer Jan Hus. They were remnants of the scattered 'Church of the United Brethren'. In 1722, a small company of Moravians settled in Saxony on Zinzendorf's estate. They named it Herrnhut — "the Lord's watch." It became a haven for Protestant refugees of many different denominations. It had been prophesied that God would 'place a light on these hills which will illume the whole land'. Despite an internal dispute that threatened to wreck the community in 1727, the fire of Pentecost fell. A new, living congregation was born. The Moravians were set up to become burning lights of missionary zeal whose impact, in part, was to be felt in England.

On August 25, 1727, a prayer meeting started that lasted for over 100 years, 24 hours a day. There was an incredible sense of God's Spirit released. People were healed, spiritual gifts such as prophecy and tongues manifested and an amazing sense of love and unity prevailed.

Like the Pietists, the Moravian Brethren believed that Christianity should be a "religion of the heart"—which went against the grain of the growing acceptance of Enlightenment beliefs. They emphasized experience of faith and love over doctrine, and thus were more accepting of varying denominational differences.

Visiting Copenhagen in 1731 to attend the coronation of King Christian VI, Zinzendorf met a converted slave from the West Indies, Anthony Ulrich. The man was looking for someone to go back to his homeland to preach the gospel to black slaves, including his sister and brother. Zinzendorf raced back to Herrnhut to find men to go. Two immediately volunteered, becoming the first Moravian missionaries, and the first Protestant missionaries of the modern era, antedating William Carey, who is often called "the father of modern missions", by sixty years.

Within two decades, Zinzendorf sent missionaries around the globe to Greenland, Lapland, Georgia, Surinam, Africa's Guinea Coast, South Africa, Amsterdam's Jewish quarter, Algeria, the native North Americans, Ceylon, Romania, and Constantinople. More than seventy missionaries from a community of fewer than six hundred answered the call. By the time Zinzendorf died in 1760 in Herrnhut, the Moravians had sent out at least 226 missionaries.

Zinzendorf's influence is felt much wider than in the Moravian Church. His emphasis on the "religion of the heart" deeply influenced John Wesley.

Late in the seventeenth century, one of the most significant and influential people from the Catholic spirituality fold was Jeanne Guyon, known as Madame Guyon (1648 – 1717). She wrote numerous books on spiritual devotion, most notably and perhaps the most influential on future generations was *Experiencing the Depths of Jesus Christ*. This book had a profound impact on Zinzendorf and the Moravians, as well as, Wesley and the Holiness movement that emerged out of Methodism and Watchman Nee who made it required reading for all members of his "little flock" in twentieth century China.

THE GREAT AWAKENING

In 1690, the total population of the American Colonies was about 250,000, almost exclusively British. At the beginning of the eighteenth century, European Protestants began to arrive in large numbers, Huguenots, Mennonites and Dutch Calvinists. There was also a large influx of German Lutherans. Many of whom were invited by William Penn to join his colony Pennsylvania. By the middle of the century, there were 70,000 Germans in the colony alone and over 200,000 in America. However, churches had become stagnant and much of the pioneering zeal had died. Moral respectability in society was more important than spiritual passion in the church.

Early signs of revival appeared amongst isolated groups in New England, but the breakthrough began in 1733 in Northampton, in a church led by Jonathan Edwards (1703 – 1758). Many were converted when the Spirit of God fell, with accounts of love, joy and distress. This outpouring occurred in a context where Edwards, one of the leading figures, also became famous for his sermon entitled, "Sinners in the Hands of an Angry God." The revival peaked in 1740 then George Whitefield (1714 – 1770) arrived on a six-week tour. When churches refused him, Whitefield took to the open air. Over the next three years, churches up and down the east coast were affected, society was changed and a new sense of social responsibility was imparted. Whitefield commented, *"The reason why congregations have been so dead is because dead men preach to them."*

At a time when unbelief was becoming fashionable and many clergy preached an empty moralism, God was raising up a new generation of people who took the truth out into the needy world. John and Charles Wesley were Anglicans from Lincolnshire, England whose father was a rector of the local parish church. John Wesley (1703 – 1791) was ordained in the Church of England in 1725. On returning to Oxford, he became one of the founding members of a group who called themselves the 'Holy Club'. Later they were ridiculed and were called Methodists, along with his brother Charles and another clergyman, George Whitefield. In 1735, the brothers went to America as missionaries. On the ship with them was a group of Moravian missionaries whose lives deeply touched the Wesleys. In America, they were not successful in their evangelistic activity. John Wesley said, *"I went to America to convert the Indians, but oh! – who shall convert me."* On their return to England in 1738, both were to be greatly influenced again by the Moravians. At a meeting on 24th May that year in Aldersgate, London, John Wesley had a life-changing experience. He described the event by writing that his heart was 'strangely warmed'. The assurance of salvation he so desperately sought was found. His younger brother Charles preceded him in his conversion by three days, and Whitefield by several years. From this point onward, they were committed to spreading the good news of salvation. At a communion service on 13 August, *'the Holy Spirit himself made them one.'* John Wesley described himself as, *'A brand plucked from the fire.'* The three of them had a profound experience of God that was about to change the world of the church in the eighteenth century. They were soon ridiculed the more and condemned as 'enthusiasts'. The origin of the word in Greek describes someone being 'in God'. A good description.

Where pulpits were open to them, they preached there. If not, they preached in the marketplace, on the public commons or in fields. The working classes, the unchurched and untouched heard and responded to the gospel as never before, with crowds of 20–30,000 attending their meetings. They were opposed and abused, but thousands turned to Christ. John Wesley traveled some 5,000 miles a year on horseback, and would stop several times a day to preach to whoever would listen. Not for nothing has Wesley been called 'God's horseman.' He said, '*I look upon all the world as my parish*'. The revival touched people's lives and the moral tone of the nation began to change significantly, socially and politically.

Converts were gathered into societies alongside local parish churches. They were not received by the Church of England and eventually formed the Methodist Church, where John Wesley's strong administrative ability was put to great use. The established church was not left untouched, however, and many excellent preachers came to the fore. Music played a very important part in the revival, Isaac Watts, John Newton and others wrote many hymns, but overshadowing them all was Charles Wesley who wrote some 7,000 hymns, many on the back of his horse.

George Whitefield was greatly used by God during this time. He was an outstanding preacher especially in the open air. He was commanding, persuasive, fervent, but plain speaking. He was a prolific traveller, going many times to America. He visited Wales, where along with Howell Harris, the Welsh Revival of 1738–1742 broke out. In Scotland in

1742,Whitefield was present when the Cambuslang Revival began. Sadly, he parted company with the Wesleys over predestination and the differences were never settled.

In America, revolution was in the air and in 1776, Independence was declared. This largely halted the spiritual fire of the Awakening. Amidst all the negativity and questioning, fresh theological thinking was provoked, however, and Christianity strengthened and fresh missionary activity began.

Political ambitions and trade stimulated much of early mission. The Roman Catholic Church had been sending missionaries from Europe to South America since the sixteenth century. The colonial powers also sent missionaries worldwide, wherever their armies and trade interests lay. It was the Moravians, however, who over a period of 150 years sent 2,170 missionaries all over the world. Their self-sacrifice, love and total commitment to evangelism inspired many, and are unparalleled in the history of mission.

THE MODERN MISSIONARY MOVEMENT

A Northamptonshire shoemaker William Carey (1761–1834) was a Baptist minister at twenty-five. He was gifted in languages and the natural sciences. An ardent collector of data, Carey was influenced by Captain Cook's serialised travels. Gripped by 'the great commission' of Matt 28:19, he published in 1792, a book with a typically long eighteenth century title that is shortened to *Enquiry*, which was a call to missionary endeavour. Despite opposition from his local Baptist leaders, the Baptist Missionary Society was founded and Carey became its pioneer and first missionary. He left for India in 1794 with his family and amidst great difficulties and personal tragedy, laboured there with great devotion for the rest of his life. He translated and studied the sacred Hindu books to understand their culture and confront pagan practices. He made twenty-four Bible translations, created sixty missionary posts and trained native leaders. This was his amazing legacy, along with thousands of converts, mission schools and an Agricultural Society. He preached on the importance of mission with the stirring words *"Expect great things from God; attempt great things for God."*

In 1818, Carey began a college in Serampore that was designed to train Indians, both non-Christian and Christian. It became a great institution and means of reaching the unsaved. When Carey died at the age of seventy-two in June 1834, there was a strong Baptist community in India. Carey in his lifetime had himself translated the Bible into forty-four Indian languages, whilst also compiling numerous dictionaries and grammars. Within fifty years of Carey's death, there were half million Indian Christians.

An American Baptist, Adoniram Judson (1788 - 1850) founded the first American Missionary Society in Burma in 1795. The London Missionary Society began in 1795 and sent missionaries to the South Pacific and Africa where one of its most famous sons was David Livingstone who opened up much of Africa to the gospel in the 1850's.

The British and Foreign Bible Society founded in 1804 was responsible for publishing Bibles for these newly emerging Christian groups. By 1907, 204 million Bibles had been published and by 1975, 250 million Bibles per year were being produced.

At the close of the eighteenth century, many denominations were stirred into action. Agencies aimed at promoting Christian work were created, amongst them numerous missionary societies. Hudson Taylor (1832 – 1905) founded the China Inland Mission in 1866. This was the first of the interdenominational faith missions. They were to play an important part in world evangelisation in the nineteenth century, following Carey's methods of training indigenous leaders and pastors. Most of the other early missions, however, failed to follow Carey's methods and superimposed on the new converts their own particular brands of denominationalism and religious practice and rules. The colonial powers, especially the British Empire, exported their own culture and tradition. These things were often forced on indigenous peoples with bloody results. In time, however, some societies began to change their emphasis. As they became more liberal, the 'good works' of agriculture, education and medical care replaced the gospel. The legacy of this approach to missionary activity has created an extremely religious and legalistic church culture in many countries in Africa, Asia and South America.

The world at that time was going through unprecedented changes. Market and population explosions forced great change. The Industrial Revolution was in full swing. Factories replaced the fields, rural slums became urban slums as towns grew and the urban society developed. Blake's 'Dark Satanic Mills' and Dickens' 'Coke-town' evoked pictures of machines, chimneys and billowing smoke. The established church was slow to respond, buildings were now too small along with too few clergy. Others, less rigid such as the 'Methodists', were more successful. The result was that the churches became associated with class. The evangelical revival was ailing spiritually, but groups of godly people were still active.

One of the great Christian social reformers at this time was William Wilberforce (1759–1833) a British politician and philanthropist. He began his political career in 1780 and was a close friend of Prime Minister William Pitt. In 1785, he underwent a conversion experience and became an evangelical Christian within the Church of England. In 1787, he came into contact with Thomas Clarkson and a group of anti-slave trade activists. This included Granville Sharp and Hannah More who pioneered literacy work, published leaflets and started Sunday schools for working class children. They were known as the Clapham Sect and worked tirelessly to better the lot of the poor. At their suggestion, Wilberforce was persuaded to take on the cause. He became one of the leading English abolitionists, heading the parliamentary campaign against the British slave trade, which he saw through to the eventual passage of the Slave Trade Act in 1807. Wilberforce also championed many other causes and campaigns, including the Society for Suppression of Vice, Charity schools, the introduction of Christianity to India, the Church Mission Society, and the Prevention of Cruelty to Animals.

In later years, he supported the campaign for complete abolition, which eventually led to the Slavery Abolition Act in 1833. This act paved the way for the complete abolition of slavery in the British Empire. A tireless campaigner for the abolition of slavery, Wilberforce died just three days after hearing of the passage of the act through Parliament. He was buried in Westminster Abbey, close to his friend William Pitt.

CHAPTER ELEVEN

19th Century Challenges And Revivals

The Rationalism of the eighteenth century continued to spread into people's thinking in the nineteenth and twentieth centuries. German theologians and philosophers played a prominent role in undermining the biblical foundation of truth. In 1859, when Charles Darwin published his *Origin of Species* it opened the door to evolutionary theory. Although the idea of evolution was not new, some very damaging conclusions were now being drawn from scientific studies. The theory of man's descent from apes and evolution of all life from a single source reduced God to an unnecessary hypothesis. Genesis became myth. The whole concept of sin was doubted, as well as all that followed on from this. T. H. Huxley persuasively argued the case for evolution and gave the theory the stamp of scientific orthodoxy. Huxley coined the word 'agnosticism', expressing a state of 'not knowing'. This became a widely used to terms to describe popular doubt about the existence of God.

Owen Chadwick says that by 1885, more educated Englishmen doubted the truth of Christianity than thirty years before. Darwin's theories affected many theologians. He had challenged the foundations of Christian belief. Many did not believe that Genesis was true and as a result much of the Old Testament was viewed with suspicion. The idea of sin and fallen man were doubted, which questioned the whole necessity of the Atonement, which as a result, led to raised questions about the divinity of Jesus. In Germany at the Tubingen School of Theology, the authenticity of the New Testament was being challenged. Modernism and liberal theology were widely accepted by the end of the century. Most came to believe that science and the Bible could not be reconciled. In a debate with Bishop Samuel Wilberforce, the son of William Wilberforce, Huxley declared he would rather descend from an ape than a bishop. The radical German philosopher Friedrich Nietzsche declared that God was dead and that the belief in the Christian God was unworthy of intellectual thought.

At the same time, two very ancient copies of the New Testament were discovered from the early Christian era, Codex Vaticanus and Codex Sinaiaticus. This provoked the desire to explore the origins of Christianity and a cry went up for a new translation of the Scriptures. The committee appointed reflected the times as it contained a Jew and a Unitarian. In 1881, the Revised Version was produced. God raised up three Cambridge scholars, three bishops: Westcott, Lightfoot, and Hort who systematically rebuffed and answered all the claims of the liberal Tubingen School.

Materialism increased in the new industrial nations of Europe alongside the industrial and agrarian revolution. There followed the exploitation of the new working classes who had left the land and gathered in huge numbers in the new industrial centres. There was the breakdown of family life and grinding poverty. Agrarian reform and the growth of the cities brought major changes to whole areas. On the back of this,

Karl Marx issued his *Communist Manifesto* in 1848 that was to impact the world immeasurably.

As spiritual vitality waned in the established church, belief became moral, repressive and hypocritical. The 'Victorian Age' conjures up pictures of ritualised church going, seriousness, authority and conformity. It was also an age of doubt and discontent. Doubts had surfaced in earlier generations, but in this age, the very fabric of Christianity was being called into question.

Historical criticism questioned the validity of the Bible and in Europe an attack on Christianity by eminent philosophers in the universities all added to the debate and controversy. Back in England at Oxford University (1861), seven Anglicans published *Essays and Reviews*. This was an attempt to reinterpret doctrine in light of new thinking. They denied the infallibility of the Bible, original sin, miracles and the resurrection. Faith was undermined and Liberalism embraced, even theological bible colleges were not unaffected.

CHRISTIAN SOCIAL CONSCIOUSNESS
AND FREE CHURCHES

Against this background of revolutionary ferment in Europe, the growth in colonialism, the slave trade and the Industrial Revolution, God was raising up a strong social consciousness among evangelicals.

Nineteenth century evangelicals began to address the needs of children. Robert Raikes founded the Sunday School Movement. Dr. Barnardo and C.H. Spurgeon started homes for orphans. The Boys Brigade and Boy Scouts began towards the end of the century. The needs of adults were addressed in the founding of the Young Men's Christian Association (YMCA) in 1844. The National Temperance League was established to combat the evils of drinking.

Prisons were reformed after Elizabeth Fry (1780 - 1845), a Quaker from Norwich, raised public awareness by her visits to prison hulks and goals. She established the first night shelter in London for the homeless. Lord Shaftesbury (1801 - 1885) was perhaps the greatest nineteenth century evangelical political reformer. As a member of Parliament, he sponsored the Ten Hour Act in 1847 and the Factory Act in 1874, which vastly improved working conditions. He campaigned against the use of women and children in mines and promoted the Chimney Sweeps Act, which forbade the use of children in this highly dangerous work. He gave away a fortune and served on many mission boards.

The non-conformist groups that became known as the Free Churches grew up in the seventeenth and eighteenth centuries. The Baptists had seen rapid growth in seventeenth century and were divided between Particular and General Baptists over the issue of grace and predestination. The Baptist Union was founded in 1813 in the UK and separated from the General Baptists. The Congregationalists were independents who broke away from the Anglicans over the autonomy of the local church. They were founded in seventeenth century and became strongly identified with the separatists and puritans. Presbyterians like the Congregationalists were sixteenth century Puritans, separatists whose churches were governed by elders. The Church of Scotland is Presbyterian. The Quakers or the Religious Society of Friends, followers of George Fox a seventeenth century puritan are non-militant pacifists. The Methodists separated from the Church of England in the eighteenth century but were not opposed to establishment. The Methodists in their turn split into denominational factions. By the end of the nineteenth century, the number of new denominations was staggering.

Emancipation of the non-conformists in Great Britain came slowly through the nineteenth century. In 1828, the repeal of the Test and Corporation Act allowed dissenters to participate in government but universities were still closed to them. Marriages were not permitted except in the Church of England buildings or burials outside of Church of England graveyards.

Tʜᴇ Sᴇᴄᴏɴᴅ Gʀᴇᴀᴛ Aᴡᴀᴋᴇɴɪɴɢ ɪɴ Aᴍᴇʀɪᴄᴀ

Up to 1800, the Protestant Churches in America were regrouping and reorganising after the break with Britain. There was a flow of population westwards over the Appalachian mountains down the Ohio to the Mississippi River and then by 1840, the rush to the Pacific began. During the first half of the nineteenth century, the churches were engaged not only in a 'conquest of the west' but also in a re-conquest of the East as part of a single surge of new religious life and activity. An initial reaction of the Protestant churches to the need for action was a renewed emphasis upon the tried and proved approach of revivalistic preaching. This led to the Second Great Awakening for two generations after 1800.

There had been earlier revivals in Hampden-Sydney and Washington Colleges in Virginia in 1787. In 1802, the Yale Chapel sermons of Timothy Dwight, the son in law of Jonathan Edwards, resulted in a third of the students being converted. Dwight commanded respect amongst the 'old Calvinists' and under his leadership the moderate anti-revivalists came into the revivalist camp. Among the students were Lyman Beecher and Nathaniel W. Taylor who became prominent in the anti-slavery movement. The revival spread to several other colleges. The new revivalism was markedly different from revivalism of the first Awakening under Jonathan Edwards when the outpouring of the Spirit was a by-product of faithful preaching. In the Second Awakening, preachers sought to provoke a revival by utilising 'means' that caused the hearers to make a decision and to make it right. Revival became a technique rather than a spontaneous and sovereign move of God.

Revivals in the 'wild west', that is over the Appalachian mountains took place among a moving and floating population were the need was for quick decisions. They put the emphasis on emotional rather than intellectual response. This was typical in Kentucky and Tennessee. Camp meetings became a feature of frontier evangelism. In 1800, at the Red River in Tennessee, Thomas McGready held a meeting that stirred up a large number of backwoodsmen. It was vastly emotional and extravagant, but they loved it. In July 1801, 10,000 turned out to Cane Ridge for a camp meeting. To get an idea of the numbers involved, Lexington, the biggest town in Kentucky, only had a population of 1,795 people. It was reported that over 3,000 were "slain in the Spirit' at one time. There was incredible confusion with various speakers all going at once. It was very emotional. But for all the excesses, church membership grew and morality increased. In Kentucky in 1800 to 1803, the Baptists increased by 10,000 members as did Methodists. But the Presbyterians were split into 3 sections over the whole issue of camp meetings. By 1811, camp meetings were exclusively Methodist with 400 meetings scattered throughout the country. Gradually, they became more dignified and orderly and eventually became conference centres or summer resorts.

Charles Finney (1792-1875) was converted in New York in 1821. Beginning his ministry in Jefferson County, he began to preach a type of gospel that aroused the whole community and soon brought down upon him the censures of his brethren in the ministry. By 1824, he was in North and Central New York State. Hundreds were being converted and revival was spreading. 1826 to 1828 saw him preaching all over New England. His most remarkable revivals were those in Rochester where in the 30's, 40's and 50's, great campaigns were conducted and nearly three thousand converts were secured. The controversial features of Finney's revivals were his 'New Measures'. His tactics were those of his training as a trial lawyer. He referred to the wicked as 'you' instead of 'they' and the 'convicted' came forward to the 'anxious' bench. His main motivation was to take revivalism from rural to urban situations. Services were held every night that went on for hours. This was called the 'protracted meeting' - lasting in a community for several weeks. Nearly every town was affected and by the 1840's Robert Baird noted that revivals had become 'a constant part of the religious system'. The camp meetings had come to town! To such extent that *he who should oppose himself to revivals as such would be regarded by most of our evangelical Christians as an enemy to spiritual religion itself.*"

THE REACTION TO REVIVAL AND
THE EMERGENCE OF CULTS.

The reaction to this revivalism varied. Unitarians and Universalists emerged at this time. The roots of Unitarianism went back to the liberal tendencies that developed in reactions to the first Great Awakening, which was a steady drift toward greater emphasis upon the human role in redemption. Boston seemed to be the main centre. Kings Chapel in Boston went Unitarian after Independence through lack of Anglican clergy. Unitarian was the faith of well-to-do urban New Englanders who rejected the notion of human depravity. Universalism arose amongst the less urbane rural people who were revolted by the excesses of the Revivalists and their emphasis on damnation.

In Upstate New York, revivals had swept back and forth across the area. Finney had his greatest successes in this area, particularly in Rochester in 1826. Along with this, the area spawned a number of alternative groups including the Church of the Latter Day Saints known as Mormons. The Millerite craze, spiritualism and various communities of Shakers all had their roots in this area. The whole region of Upstate New York became known as the "Burnt Over" district.

Joseph Smith (1805-44) settled in Palmyra, New York. His father was a seer of visions and digger of hidden treasure. Joseph Jnr. apparently had his first vision in 1820. By 1827, in one of his visions, a supposed visitation by the "angel Moroni" had revealed to Smith the site of a hidden box of golden plates which was to be the Bible for the western world but it was written in 'Reformed Egyptian' tongue. Along with the golden plates was an accompanying set of stones that helped Smith read them. Smith translated the plates behind a conveniently placed curtain. When he finished the translation, the angel Moroni removed them from human view apparently. As a result in 1830, the book of Mormon was published in Palmyra. It claims to be the story of ancient American Nephites and Lamanites, known then as the Red Indians. Following persecution, the Mormons gradually moved or rather were moved west to Ohio. In 1836, Brigham Young joined them and became one of the twelve apostles. The Mormons moved on to Missouri then to the Illinois from 1840 to 1846. In July 1843, Smith introduced polygamy into their religion. The leaders Hyrum and Smith were put in prison in 1844, but an angry mob broke into the prison and shot them both. Two years later under the leadership of Brigham Young, they moved out to Utah where they founded a Mormon state and Salt Lake City.

Another figure who began a new sect was a New England Baptist farmer named William Miller. He fixed the date of the second coming by calculations from Daniel and Revelation for sometime between March 21, 1843 and March 21, 1844. In August 1831, he began to warn the people of America. Soon, he was invited to preach all over the United States. When 1843 dawned, emotions were white hot. On March 21st, hilltops were crowded across the US and nothing unusual happened. Quick recalculations put the second coming of Jesus to be scheduled for October 22, 1844. Again, hilltops were crowded and graveyards packed awaiting the resurrection of the dead, but the day passed. This ended the prophecy of the exact day but the advent expectation went on. In 1845, the Millerites also known as Adventists were organised into a loose organization. In 1846, the Seventh Day Adventists separated from the Millerites over observance of the Jewish sabbath.

Hundreds of disillusioned Millerites joined the Shakers, who believed that Christ had already appeared for the second time in the person of Mother Ann Lee. The "Adventists'" impact was greatest on the Shaker villages in Ohio, Massachusetts and New Hampshire.

In 1847 in Rochester, New York, three sisters: Margaret, Kate and Leah Fox heard rapping noises in their home that were claimed to be directed by some spiritual intelligence. The sisters began holding meetings where these spirits communicated from beyond the grave. Spiritualism had arrived. Gradually spiritualism grew in public favour and by 1855, there were over 2,000,000 believers in the USA. Much later in life, one of the sisters confessed that the rapping noises were in fact nothing more than her creaking knee joints and the whole phenomena a total fabrication.

The revivalists were mostly postmillennialists believing that Jesus would return after a thousand years of peace and church growth. They thought therefore that the church needed to help bring about godliness in society. They believed that where there was revival there must also be reform. Society was scrutinized. Scarcely any area of American society was untouched: temperance, Sabbath observance, world peace, profanity, vice, women's rights, slavery, prison conditions, and education were all on the agenda of revivalist social reform. Revivals provided the impetus for the battle against sin. Reform would bring on the Kingdom of God and righteousness. Finney said, *"Every member must work or quit. There are no honorary members."* In 1831, the publication the 'New York Evangelist' announced that it was devoted to revivals, doctrinal discussion and religious intelligence. In 1835, it added practical godliness and in 1837, human rights. Economic problems were first thought to be solvable by individual conversion, but by 1851, urban renewal through low rents, clean buildings and healthy surroundings were advocated.

The issue of slavery soon took the attention of revivalists and the enthusiasm of revivalism was applied to abolition of slavery. The slavery controversy that followed shook America to its roots. Repentance of sin for any personal involvement in and support of the slave system was taught. The main exponent was Theo Dwight Weld (1803 –1895), a revivalist preacher. As the abolitionist's voice grew louder, so did its opposition. The Southern Champions became highly vocal. Pro-slavery sentiment in the South and the anxiety of a growing minority status of the slave holding states added to the fierceness of Southern resistance to the abolitionists. Southern clergy held that God ordained slavery. Perfectionism was gaining much ground in the North and taught that all one needed to do to become perfect was to abolish sin. Slavery was viewed as the greatest sin. New York State became the centre of the anti-slavery movement coupled with perfectionism. Also, the Methodists in

New York State were fiercely anti-slavery. In 1843 at Utica, a Wesleyan Methodist Church was formed which included abolitionism as one of its tests of membership.

Gradually, all the churches were split over the issue of slavery roughly between North and South. Political division followed and by 1860, civil war had broken out. Both the Union soldiers and the Confederates sang hymns of revival. The children of famous revivalists were hotly abolitionist. Lyman Beecher's daughter, Harriet Beecher Stowe was the author of *Uncle Tom's Cabin*, which was a very powerful novel that exposed the evils of slavery. Southern Baptists split away from the United Baptists in the North over the slavery controversy.

RENEWAL AND REVIVAL IN BRITAIN.

Early in the 1800's, news reached Britain of the camp meetings in the United States. English Methodists were very interested. Hugh Bourne became an early convert to the camp meeting style of evangelism. Bourne held a prayer meeting in Mow Cop Cheshire at 6:00am on May 31, 1807. Thousands attended these prayer meetings, but they were hardly a camp meeting in the American sense. In July 1807, the Methodist Conference said that camp meetings were highly improper and disclaimed any connections. Hugh Bourne refused to accept this judgment and continued to preach in open-air meetings and fairs. Within a year, he was turned out of the Methodist Society but continued to preach. In 1812, he formed the Society of Primitive Methodists. They continued to hold open-air meetings and had many conversions. By 1850, there were 150,000 members. They were characterised by aggressive evangelism and a strong social conscience. Their greatest converts in the mid century were C.H. Spurgeon and William Booth.

Wales experienced revivals regularly in one area or another and were accompanied by the Welsh phenomenon of 'moliannu' or praising. They affected all the free churches. In five years, beginning in 1816, Baptists in Wales gained 8,000 members. Scotland was dominated by the revivals led by James and Robert Haldane which spread all over Scotland with amazing results even to the 'heathen' Hebradian Isles.

The American revival spread to England where between 1860 and 1862 there were one million converts. One of the converts of Finney's preaching in America was D. L. Moody. Moody teamed up with Ira Sankey and together they led extensive campaigns from 1870 onwards during which thousands more were saved. Moody came to England in 1873 and spent two years preaching and seeing amazing results. It is reported that he preached to over 100 million people. The Holiness movement grew out of these revivals and churches committed to New Testament simplicity and holiness came into being e.g. the Churches of Christ. The Keswick Convention started in 1875. C. T. Studd (1862 - 1931) was converted in 1877 at a Moody meeting and along with other Cambridge students went to China with the China Inland Mission. He eventually founded WEC, the World-wide Evangelisation Crusade.

Catholic 'Renewal' took the form of Anglicans becoming more Catholic through the Oxford Movement in the 1840s. A group of Anglican clerics met at Oxford University. Their desire was to get back to the grass roots of the early church, with an emphasis on the sacraments and church tradition including apostolic succession. They restored a sense of reverence and dignity in worship and encouraged the restoring of church architecture and ritual. They were more 'medieval' in nature and led ultimately to being described as Anglo-Catholics in the Church of England. When in 1841, the vicar of St. Mary's Oxford, John Henry Newman, wrote

Tract 90, stating that the 39 Articles could be interpreted in a Catholic sense, he created an uproar. Soon after, he left the Anglican Church and became a Catholic. He was later ordained as a Roman Catholic and became a Cardinal and after his death was canonized as a saint.

In Rome, Jesuits dominated the papacy. They were rapidly losing control of their land holdings in Italy and sought to strengthen its spiritual hold. In 1854, the doctrine of the Immaculate Conception of the Blessed Virgin Mary was defined. This refers to the sinless conception of Mary by her parents and teaches the sinlessness of Mary herself in her role as the mother of God. Then in 1870, as Pope Pius IX retreated into the Vatican City when Garibaldi unified Italy, the doctrine of Papal Infallibility was defined which means that the Pope speaking 'ex cathedra' that is in his official capacity cannot be wrong. He had just lost all his temporal power and land holdings and in response, reasserted his spiritual authority over the Catholic world.

William and Catherine Booth founded The Salvation Army in 1878. William Booth (1829 - 1912) was a staunch Arminian who was converted through the Primitive Methodists. The movement began in a tent in Whitechapel, in east London and grew into a powerful, spirit-filled movement. Salvationists were abused, attacked, even killed, but were fearless, especially among the working classes. They were strongly opposed by the mainline churches. Shaftesbury called them *"a trick of the devil who was trying to make Christianity ridiculous."* Men and women enlisted as singing soldiers, identifying with the task of getting to people's hearts before their social conditions. They planted centres known as Citadels throughout the country and touched the untouchables. In 1885, Booth and the Salvation Army were instrumental in spearheading a national petition to protect children from being forced against their will into prostitution. In 1890, Booth published 'In Darkest England and the Way Out' and sought to show that the English were as much enslaved as the Africans. By the time of his death, the 'Army' was worldwide.

Outside of the established church, there was growth and spiritual vitality. In 1854 at aged 19, Charles Haddon Spurgeon (1834 – 1892) became a Baptist pastor. His direct, witty preaching, which some thought irreverent led to many conversions and drew vast congregations. He planted churches and trained nine hundred ministers in thirty years. He was called the 'Prince of Preachers' and was probably the greatest preacher of the nineteenth century. He founded a training college for Baptists known initially as The Pastor's College, now known as Spurgeon's College, the author being one of its graduates. Spurgeon also established a work among orphans and set up institutions that became known as Spurgeon's Homes.

Another group that emerged, in the century under the leadership of J.N. Darby in Dublin in 1827, was the Brethren. Divisions within the Brethren movement led to a breakaway group who shunned all contact with other Christians and the world. They became known as the Exclusive Brethren.

Men such as George Muller led an offshoot that began in Plymouth in 1830, and spread to Bristol. This branch of the Brethren was known as the Plymouth Brethren.

Muller became the Director of an orphanage in Bristol, England, and cared for 10,024 orphans in his lifetime. As part of the care he gave to the orphans, he provided an education to the children, to the point where he was accused of raising the poor above their natural station in life.

He also established over one hundred schools, which offered Christian education to over 120,000 children, many of them orphans.

Muller wrote in his journal known as *Narratives* that, "*the word of God alone is our standard of judgment in spiritual things; that it can be explained only by the Holy Spirit; and that in our day, as well as in former times, he is the teacher of his people. The office of the Holy Spirit I had not experimentally understood before that time. Indeed, of the office of each of the blessed persons, in what is commonly called the Trinity, I had no experimental apprehension. I had not before seen from the Scriptures that the Father chose us before the foundation of the world; that in him that wonderful plan of our redemption originated, and that he also appointed all the means by which it was to be brought about. Further, that the Son, to save us, had fulfilled the law, to satisfy its demands, and with it also the holiness of God; that he had borne the punishment due to our sins, and had thus satisfied the justice of God. And, further, that the Holy Spirit alone can teach us about our state by nature, show us the need of a Saviour, enable us to believe in Christ, explain to us the Scriptures, help us in preaching.*"

Muller, like many in the nineteenth century, was beginning to see truth that had been forgotten by the church. His life was a remarkable example of living by faith, dependant of the promptings of the Holy Spirit with a growing understanding of God's heart as a Father.

The Holy Spirit Rediscovered

Throughout the nineteenth century, there was a growing understanding that the work and doctrine of the Holy Spirit was a neglected truth. In Scotland in 1830, individuals experienced an outpouring and tongues. George MacDonald began to experience a flow of spiritual gifts including healings. In London, Edward Irving (1792 – 1834) was leading a church that became a centre of Holy Spirit activity, prayer meetings and manifestations. Born out of this emphasis came the Apostolic church, the earliest of what was to become the Pentecostal churches.

Slowly, teachers and theologians began to define the doctrine of the Baptism of the Holy Spirit. Significant alongside Edward Irving and Charles Finney was Phoebe Palmer (1807 -1874) an influential theologian based in New York. She held meetings in her home and taught large numbers to seek what was described as a second blessing. Her teaching replaced the Wesleyan terminology of sanctification with baptism in the Holy Spirit.

At one of D.L. Moody's meetings in London in 1875, the Holy Spirit fell on the congregation and there was prophecy and tongues. This began to happen in a number of meetings led by significant leaders who all collectively prepared the way for the outpourings that came in the early twentieth century.

This was an age of enormous diversity in theological thinking, speculation of liberalism and painstaking historical and biblical criticism. There were great advances in scientific knowledge and rapid population growth. The church was entrenched in its ideas over a 'spiritual' or 'social' gospel and the arguments grounded on and on. Through all of this, the belief remained amongst liberal humanists and supporters of a 'social Christianity', that a better world (the Kingdom of God), was at hand. Meanwhile, other parts of 'the church' were continuing to declare the gospel in all its fullness, seeing many conversions and new churches established.

As the church entered the twentieth century, many Christians felt that the millennial age was about to dawn. The vast colonial empires of Britain, France, Spain, Russia and Germany ruled the world. America was a sleeping giant and Japan a rising dragon. The previous century had seen amazing industrial and scientific advance. Mankind was feeling sophisticated and adult. The religious intolerance and social barbarism of previous centuries was replaced by a tolerance and gentility that many felt was the dawn of a new age for mankind. Minor colonial wars had upset the peace of the world but generally the world saw ahead an unlimited age of peace, progress and contentment.

Optimism was the mark of the first fourteen years of the century. All this disappeared as a shot was fired in Sarajevo in 1914. The assassination of the Austrian Archduke Ferdinand marked the start of the First World War in which over 10 million Europeans would lose their lives.

Revival begins again in Wales

Before the outbreak of the First World War, there were signs that God was doing something new. In Wales (1904–1905), beginning with gatherings for prayer and the constant call for revival, fresh outpourings of the Holy Spirit broke out. One of the key preachers in this was a young theological student Evan Roberts (1878 – 1951). The Spirit of God came and wonderful experiences were related, many were converted and baptized in the Spirit. Elsewhere, in different parts of England and Scotland, revival was also reported. News spread across to North America where protracted prayer meetings and "tarrying" were the precursors of revival. Its influence was felt in Africa, India and the Far East. Sadly, this revival was criticized so much that Roberts burnt out and withdrew completely from ministry and the revival ended. However, before its culmination, the Welsh revival influenced some preachers in America who were to see a great outpouring in Los Angeles.

In Los Angeles in 1906, revival began. A revival typified inwardly by baptism in the Spirit and outwardly by speaking in tongues and the accompanying spiritual gifts, including healing. On April 14, 1906, at the Azusa Street Mission, a revival broke out that birthed the modern Pentecostal movement. Hundreds of Christians from all over North America visited Los Angeles, followed by people from Britain, Europe and elsewhere. The Los Angeles Times reported the events as thus, "*the devotees of the weird doctrine practice the most fanatical rites, preach the wildest theories and work themselves into a state of mad excitement. Night is made hideous in the neighbourhood by the howlings of the worshippers, who spend hours swaying back and forth in a nerve-racking attitude of prayer and supplication. They claim to have the gift of tongues and to be able to understand the babel.*" During the meeting on April 19th, the building physically shook and the meeting reached near hysteria. At that exact moment, the great San Francisco earthquake was devastating the city several hundred miles to the North.

Rev. William Seymour (1870 – 1922) led this revival. Seymour was a black Holiness pastor. The meetings were filled with prayer and Seymour refused to do anything until he was convinced he was full of the Holy Spirit. Meetings lasted from mid morning until the early hours daily and continued for three years. Throughout, visitors came from all over the world and carried the message back home. By 1908, fifty countries were experiencing similar outpourings. Soon, those carrying the message were being referred to as Pentecostals. Various expressions of this move were grouping into denominations such as the Assemblies of God. By 1914, there were Pentecostals in every American city and every country that had been influenced by the Azusa Street outpouring. Within fourteen years, there were at least twenty-five separate denominations. The mission church itself on Azusa Street, however, declined into a small local black congregation.

There was widespread criticism from the established churches worldwide. German Lutherans went so far as to condemn Pentecostals as satanic and Satan's last vomit. This blocked the move of the Spirit in Europe for more than a generation.

The outbreak of the First World War in 1914 did much to damage Christianity as a whole and was a severe blow to the liberals and their emphasis on the increasing goodness of man. Nonetheless, the fires of revival spread, with people from all nations bringing back from America the teaching and experience of Spirit baptism and speaking in tongues. Pentecostalism arrived in Britain, at first through early 'Crusades'. In

1910, God raised up two influential brothers from Wales, George and Stephen Jeffreys who saw thousands converted and many amazing miracles of healing. They also planted churches. The Jeffreys' brothers formed the Elim Alliance in 1915. The Apostolic Church founded in 1916 appointed Ephesians 4 type ministries but within a generation had become institutionalised.

Two women who had powerful healing ministries in this period were Maria Woodworth Etter (1844 – 1924) and Aimee Semple McPherson (1890 – 1944). Etter was an important forerunner to the Pentecostal movement and after Azusa Street, she experienced increased anointing and quite unusual for the era experienced a great sense of unity with most groups. McPherson drew inspiration from Etter and battled huge opposition as a woman. However, her meetings across America were packed and the presence of God was palpable. She built the Angelus Temple in Los Angeles that seated 5,000. In 1922, she preached what is believed to be the first radio broadcast sermon. In 1927, she formally incorporated the International Church of the Foursquare Gospel.

One of the earliest European expressions of Pentecostalism was in Sweden. The first Pentecostal church was the Filadelfia Church in Stockholm. Pastored by Lewi Pethrus, this congregation, originally Baptist was expelled from the Baptist Union of Sweden in 1913 for doctrinal differences. As of 2005, the Swedish Pentecostal movement had approximately 90,000 members in nearly 500 congregations. Swedish Pentecostals have been very missionary-minded and have established churches in many countries. In Brazil, for example, churches founded by the Swedish Pentecostal mission claim several million members.

Amongst others powerfully used by God was Smith Wigglesworth

Evangelist !

(1859 – 1947) who had a remarkable ministry of preaching and healing. He also had an international ministry. He ministered in the United States, Sweden, Australia, New Zealand, South Africa, the Pacific Islands, India, Ceylon, and several countries in Europe. Wigglesworth made a commitment to God that he would not sleep at night before he had won a soul for Christ every day. He claimed that on one occasion he could not sleep because he had not met this commitment, and that he went out into the night and met an alcoholic to whom he spoke and persuaded to become a believer. Wigglesworth is considered one of the most influential evangelists in the early history of Pentecostalism and is also credited with helping give the movement a large religious audience.

1900 - 1950

The first half of the twentieth century was a period of unprecedented change throughout the whole world. In 1900, the imperial expansion of the European powers was at its height and the newly established countries of the Orient, in the America's and Africa were almost entirely governed by the European colonial nations.

In the early part of the twentieth century, the Missionary societies were buoyed along on the tide of missionary enthusiasm that had marked the nineteenth century and were joined by a new flood of missionaries from the Pentecostal churches. Along with this, they carried many of the weaknesses of the past also. Imperialism and colonialism were still the accepted systems of government in the missionary areas. One of the greatest weaknesses for the missionary societies was that they were considered by the peoples amongst whom they worked as agents of colonialism, the vendors of a western religion. This was considered to be just another by-product of colonialism. Among the Protestant missions this was particularly true with missionaries regarding Europe as their home and with a sense of superiority, inflicting on their new converts western forms of Christianity and culture. Western music and art were employed as the media of expression in the church. Western clothes and clerical dress were imposed upon the native converts and ministers. The Gothic style of architecture was employed in the raising of church buildings all over the missionary areas. There was a curious smell of imperialism around the mission stations and compounds.

The structures that they built were based upon the denominational ideals of the home countries and very few attempts were made to unite the new Christians in a national church. A native of North China might on his conversion find himself to be a Plymouth Brother or an American Southern Baptist. Neither was any real attempt made to make the church in the mission areas truly indigenous. Few were trained to be leaders or pastors simply because theirs was such a narrow view of imperialism. The British Empire was thought to be going on for many more years.

In 1910, the Edinburgh Missionary Conference did much to establish closer links between the societies and a greater degree of cooperation on the mission field ensued. The 1914-18 war rocked the world to its foundations as so many of the old ideas and values were shattered. Nationalism in the missionary countries began to be a major issue. The churches in the missionary areas began to be called 'Younger Churches' and their leadership was slowly handed over to nationals with missionaries working alongside as colleagues. The extensive programmes of educational and medical aid were continued with many of the new techniques and treatments being introduced into the emerging countries. The Missionary Societies began to de-westernise their missions. The cultures of the peoples they sought to help were examined and many genuine attempts were made to relate the Christian faith to their own cultures.

THE CHALLENGES OF WORLD WAR,
FASCISM AND COMMUNISM

The First World War destroyed the hopes and optimism of the world. The church in the twentieth century was to face even bigger challenges: Communism, Fascism, Individualism, and Humanism. When the Second World War broke out in 1939, many people became disillusioned and lost their faith.

The Russian Revolution of 1917 marked the start of a battle for the life of the church in dozens of countries. The Stalinist era in the Soviet Union virtually annihilated all organised religion. Millions of Christians of all persuasions disappeared. Persecution was systematic and ruthless. Church property and resources where taken over. By 1939, the Russian church was weak and virtually extinct. A brief respite in World War II was followed by more subtle persecution after the war. Post War Eastern Europe smothered by Soviet style communism spread the attack on the church in all the satellite communist nations of Europe.

The rise of Italian Fascism in the 1920s and the outbreak of the Second World War was marked by a growing tension between the Italian State and the Papacy. There is much debate as to how involved the Pope was with the fascist government. Catholicism in Spain was traditionally allied with the conservative side in every dispute and sided with Franco against the Republicans. The fact that the church had not made a clear stand against these repressive regimes may be partly to blame for the Post War decline in Southern Europe.

National Socialism in Germany was born out of social Darwinism and racial evolution and the disorientation of Germany following its defeat in the First War. The Nazi party saw Christianity as a Jewish plot and all true Christians were targets of their attack. The Catholic and Lutheran churches of Germany tried to accommodate the increasingly hostile government. Many German church leaders already weakened by liberalism tried to remove the Jewish elements from the German church and tragically compromised with the Nazis. A Reich bishop was appointed over the church in Germany who merged the Evangelical Youth Movement with the Hitler Youth and alienated the evangelical wing of the church. Huge numbers of Christians from all groups were executed. The process was known as Kirkenkampf. Catholics suffered as much as any other group under the Nazis. Typical was Maximilian Kolbe (1894- 1941), a Polish Franciscan who volunteered to die in place of a stranger in the Nazi concentration camp of Auschwitz in Poland. He was later canonised by the Pope.

The Confessing church emerged in Germany that opposed the German-Christians. It was led by men such as Dietrich Bonheoffer (1906 – 1945) who was a German Lutheran pastor, theologian, and participant in the German Resistance movement against Nazism. He was a founding member of the Confessing church. He was involved in plots planned by members of the Abwehr, the German Military Intelligence Office, to assassinate Adolf Hitler. He was arrested in March 1943, imprisoned and eventually hung in a brutal way just before the end of World War II. Europe was purged of Christians during the 1939 - 1945 war and the church was left decimated and weakened by the persecutions and by the attack of Liberalism.

Post war decline in the traditional mainline denominations continued rapidly. Church attendance hit all time lows and it looked as if the church would almost die out in some parts of the world. The '60s were a time of

60's great moral change. Music, permissiveness, interest in other faiths and new age spirituality developed hand-in-hand along with materialism and secularism. The church did not seem to have the answers. The search for unity by mainline denominations was a major feature of post war Europe often driven by declining numbers and the need to reduce the cost of maintaining buildings rather than the desire for heart felt unity of spirit. Churches united to form the World Council of Churches in 1948. This body has been deeply involved in political activity and was not a true representative body for the worldwide church. Most evangelical groups did not join.

Brief revivals broke out in the Scottish Hebridean Islands and in the Anglican church of East Africa in the 1940s. Their influence stirred many to hunger for more.

Post war Europe was in a state of deep spiritual shock. Eastern Europe had been swallowed by Soviet style communism and experienced extensive persecution and official church compromise. In the west, there was a new liberalism abroad. Bishop Robinson published his book *Honest to God* in which he espoused the 'God is Dead' theory in 1963. Economic recovery, materialism and the prevailing humanism of the age led to drastic numerical decline in Protestant northern Europe. All main line denominations reported steady drops in membership.

Catholic entrenchment took place in their response to the mood of the age. The Assumption of the Blessed Virgin Mary was made official doctrine in 1950 at the second Vatican council. This taught that as Mary was sinless, she did not need to die but was taken up bodily, i.e. assumed, into heaven. Her assumption also provided for an explanation of her appearances at places of pilgrimage such as Lourdes. It was the logical journey's end of an erroneous doctrine that began in the early church era.

However, there was a mood of change in grass root Catholics who wanted a greater sense of openness. The Bible was made available in the vernacular, that is the local languages of the churches, and like all people exposure to the Word brought a new openness to God. The papacy under John XXIII and Paul IV became more visible. Pope John Paul II (1920 - 2005), the first non-Italian pope for centuries, was even more visible and mobile in his glass-domed pope-mobile. There was a Catholic resurgence in Poland and also an increase in the adoration of Mary. Third World Catholicism became a force within the Catholic Church and championed Liberation Theology that supported the revolutionary movements in South America. Officially, the Vatican disapproved of this approach. Finally in 2013, a Latin American cardinal became Pope Francis. This seems to have ushered in a new era for the Catholic Church. This pope uses language that is more typical of charismatic evangelicals. At his first Good Friday Mass after his elevation to the papacy he said, *"The cross is the word through which God has responded to evil in the world, a word which is love, mercy and forgiveness. It also reveals a judgment. Namely that God in judging us, loves us. Let us remember this: God judges us by loving us. If I embrace his love then I am saved. If I refuse it, then I am condemned, not by him, but by my own self, because God never condemns, he only loves and saves."* A new day indeed.

EVANGELICAL AND PENTECOSTAL RESURGENCE
AND CHARISMATIC RENEWAL

In spite of the overall decline, there were some exceptions. William Branham (1909 – 1965), a Baptist minister was at the centre of a healing ministry and revival in North America between 1946 and

1954. It is reported that over half a million conversions were recorded. He particularly moved in the spiritual gift of the word of knowledge. He influenced such people as Kenneth Hagin, Kathryn Kuhlman and Oral Roberts. An offshoot of Branham's ministry was the Latter Rain revival, which happened in Vancouver in 1948. The revival had a huge emphasis on the miraculous. However, this move was bitterly opposed by mainline Pentecostals.

A feature of the post war years was Conservative fundamentalism in the USA. The major evangelical denominations in the USA have all seen growth and 'born again Christian' is almost a fashionable label and a force to be taken into account in all American presidential elections. Large numbers of American missionaries have gone out all over the world along with the American culture.

After the war, mass evangelism through the media of radio and TV was pioneered through the USA with the most famous exponent being Billy Graham (born 1918). Graham began preaching in the style of Moody and the other great nineteenth century evangelists, but quickly adopted the TV medium in the USA, Europe and Australasia. Cable and satellite TV have opened most of the world up to his crusades. He was seen as a warm, straight-talking man, with a simple, Bible-centred message. In the 1950s, he had great success with his radio programme and televised rallies. When he arrived in England in the '50s and late '60s, packed rallies saw thousands converted. He strongly believed in integrating all new converts into local churches, but many found them to be unwelcoming. 'The Bible says...' was one of Graham's key phrases. However, his preaching did not include an emphasis on the baptism of the Holy Spirit.

Luis Palau, an Argentinean adopted a similar style and has conducted extensive crusades in Latin America. In Africa, Reinhard Bonnke has conducted major evangelistic missions. All three report hundreds of thousands responding. In Africa and South America, the church saw many added to its numbers. In Europe, however, the lapse rate of those making commitments continued to be very high.

The emergence of the teenager and the youth culture in the 50s led to Youth Evangelism on a major scale. Organisations aimed at youth have proliferated, many outside of the mainstream of church life, and all have had difficulty integrating their converts into local churches. There has been a strong emphasis on discipleship and evangelism in these groups. Most notable among them are Operation Mobilisation, Youth With A Mission, Campus Crusade for Christ, and Youth for Christ.

The Charismatic movement emerged in 1960 in Van Nuys, California as God began to pour out his Spirit on an Anglican/Episcopalian church led by Dennis Bennett. It widely influenced many main line denominations and came to be known as the Renewal. Michael Harper, a British Anglican curate who came into contact with this new move of the Spirit, was profoundly affected. In 1965, he left his parish to form The Fountain Trust to promote spiritual renewal in the United Kingdom. Many mainstream Christians from Lutheran, Methodist, Baptist, and Dutch Reformed churches were led into the 'Baptism of the Spirit' and the Renewal movement was born. Towards the end of the '60s, Roman Catholics were greatly touched as the 'move of the Spirit' began to affect nearly all churches. It became known as the Charismatic Renewal.

For some in mainstream churches, change was very slow or else resisted. The result was that many people left, and out of this came the so-called

215

'House Churches' of the 1970s. These groups were very diverse in their make-up, but possibly the largest was what came to be known as the Restoration movement. They saw what was happening as God restoring lost features of New Testament to the Church. Restorationism, as this was called, was divided by controversy over heavy shepherding and discipling in the early 1980s. All the restorationist groups are committed to seeing a revival or restoration of the so-called Ephesians 4 ministries functioning in the church. A number of streams have emerged under various apostolic teams. Covenant Ministries led by Bryn and Keri Jones were very influential in the 1970s in the UK and in South Africa but have peaked in recent years and have become relatively isolationist.

Many of these groups were more radical than the Pentecostals with much emphasis on lively Spirit led worship and body ministry. Many denominational churches were not prepared to change and as a result there was a major exodus of members from traditional churches into house churches. These began to be called New Churches by the late 1980s.

North American Charismatics have consistently influenced these streams. The Fort Lauderdale Five, including Ern Baxter, Bob Mumford, Derek Prince, Charles Simpson and Don Basham had a major input in the early 1970s and contributed greatly to the discipleship controversy. In the 1980s, John Wimber and the Vineyard movement impacted the restorationist and renewal movement among the Charismatic denominational churches through a series of major teaching conferences. In the 1990s, controversy emerged again over the so-called Kansas City Prophets and Paul Cain whom John Wimber had introduced to the world Charismatic scene. Kansas City became a major centre after Mike Bickle moved there to pastor the Kansas City Fellowship and amongst other initiatives founded the International House of Prayer, a centre for prayer and worship that operates 24/7. He brought considerable stability to the prophetic ministries based there. Bethel Church in Redding, California is one of the major centres of influence in the post Charismatic era of the twenty-first century. + Hillsong

The last half of the twentieth century has been a time of unprecedented growth in the church worldwide with the exception of the historically Christian nations of Western Europe and their former European dominated colonies such as Australia and New Zealand.

China, since the war, has seen amazing changes. The Chinese Communist take-over in 1949 resulted in the expulsion of all foreign missionaries. The official church was forcibly united under the Three Self movement. The decade of Mao's Cultural Revolution was intended to wipe out the church in China. Many were martyred and suffered. Watchman Nee (1903 - 1972) was a major voice speaking from China and encouraged the underground church to flourish. He was imprisoned in 1952 until his death in 1972. His writings still have a huge impact throughout the world. When China reopened its doors, it was found that the church was far from dead. There were reports that Charismatic church life is extensive with 25,000 a day being saved. Kevin Choy stated, in a Chinese weekly newspaper in Hong Kong, that the correct number of Protestants in China should be around 20 million, while Time Magazine recently reported 65 million. Chinese government figures admit a far higher figure than they had previously done.

The Korean Church has seen incredible growth especially among Pentecostals and Presbyterians. Paul Yongi Cho led the world's largest church of over 850,000. Goals for the decade of 2000-2010 included the establishment of some five thousand satellite churches and five hundred prayer houses, similar to Prayer Mountain. Over the past few decades, Christianity has increased dramatically in South Korea. In the year 2005, about eighteen percent of the population professed to be Protestants and around ten percent Roman Catholics. Seoul, the capital of South Korea, contains eleven of the world's twelve largest Christian congregations. South Korea is also the world's second largest missionary nation with the United States as the first nation. South Korean missionaries are particularly prevalent in 10/40 Window nations that are hostile to Westerners. In 2000, there were 10,646 Korean Protestant missionaries in 156 countries, along with a large but undisclosed number of Catholic Missionaries.

Revival broke out in Indonesia between 1970 and 1980. In Southeast Asia, communism and persecution plagued the church but since the fall of the Communist nations, a resurgence of Christian life has occurred. Huge Christian churches are now found in all Asian nations where there is freedom to practice their faith.

With the end of Communism in Europe and the collapse of the Soviet Union, the door to the gospel reopened into Eastern Europe. American missionaries in large numbers have poured into the old communist countries with their various brands of Pentecostal denominationalism. Huge numbers of commitments have been recorded, but the churches lack the resources to disciple and add the new converts to them. A huge spiritual vacuum exists which is rapidly being filled. The cults have moved into the former communist countries in a big way. The Ukraine is currently experiencing a major revival with churches being planted all over the country.

Africa has seen significant developments and is reported to be 52% 'born again' in 1990. At the beginning of the twenty-first century,

Sub Saharan Africa is being described as Christian Africa. Nigerian emigration has led to huge Nigerian churches being established in the USA and Europe. The largest church in the United Kingdom is a Nigerian congregation in east London of over 10,000.

Evangelical Lutherans from Norway were active in Ethiopia and helped established the Mekane Jesu church that now has over five million members. Revival is gaining pace in Mozambique under the influence of Roland and Heidi Baker. A recent comment on Egyptian TV by the Islamic world's leading spokesman on the spread of Islam publically stated that they have lost Africa since the Christians started raising the dead.

Pentecostal denominations have seen massive expansion in the third world since the War. In the USA, Pentecostals have invested heavily in television and Tele-evangelists such as Jimmy Swaggart and Jim Baker have risen and fallen. The largest Pentecostal denomination in the US is the Church of God in Christ. The largest Pentecostal denomination in the world, the Assemblies of God, has over 12,311 churches in the U.S. and 283,413 churches and outstations in over 200 countries, and approximately 57 million adherents worldwide. According to a spring 1998 article in Christian History, there are about 11,000 different Pentecostal or Charismatic denominations worldwide.

The size of Pentecostalism in the United States is estimated to be more than 20 million including approximately 918,000 (4%) of the Hispanic-American population. Toronto, Canada, has a large Pentecostal population. The influence of immigrants from Jamaica, Africa, Latin America, Korea and elsewhere have created diverse churches throughout the city.

In Australia, Hillsong Church led by Brian Houston is the largest church, with a membership exceeding 19,000. Many of their songs are sung in Pentecostal Churches and other denominations and their style of worship has influenced many large independent churches across the world. They are a member of the Assemblies of God denomination, which is one of the largest Pentecostal organizations in the world.

Hillsong Church

Pentecostalism was estimated to number around 115 million followers worldwide in 2000. The great majority of Pentecostals are found in developing countries, although much of their international leadership is still in North America. Pentecostalism is sometimes referred to as the "third force of Christianity". According to Christianity Today, Pentecostalism is "a vibrant faith among the poor; it reaches into the daily lives of believers, offering not only hope but a new way of living. In addition, according to a 1999 U.N. report, Pentecostal churches have been the most successful at recruiting its members from the poorest of the poor."

Latin American Pentecostal growth has been extensive with the Pentecostals fast overtaking the Catholics in numerical strength. All countries in South America report massive church growth. Argentina has produced some outstanding leaders such as Claudio Freidzon who have impacted Christianity in the western world. In 1986, Freidzon founded the King of Kings Church in Argentina, which today has a weekly attendance of over 20,000 members. Claudio Freidzon is among the foremost figures of the extraordinary revival that has been taking place in Argentina since 1992. He has also been a catalyst for the current worldwide revival. In Argentina they say, *'Before there was Toronto or Sunderland, there was Argentina.'* More than 850,000 people have attended his crusades. There have been many healings from a whole range of sicknesses and countless lives have been dramatically changed. Restoration of families has been a highlight in this revival.

American nominalism and religious scandals have brought evangelicals and Pentecostals into disrepute. Some analysts feel that American church growth has peaked. In Western Europe, resistance and declining church attendance are still alarming though the growth in the charismatic and Pentecostal churches is steady and encouraging.

A new wave of renewal broke out in Toronto in 1994 centred on a Vineyard church led by John and Carol Arnott. I will look at this in more detail in the next chapter. Suffice it to say, its influence has deeply impacted the church worldwide.

In 1996, revival broke out at Brownsville in Pensacola, Florida, which had a very strong Pentecostal flavour to it. Thousands visited from all over the world and many where deeply touched and came to repentance. Sadly, like many revivals, it petered out as controversy raged over its validity and its leaders did not carry the integrity needed to sustain a true work of God.

The rediscovery of the gifts, ministry and baptism of the Holy Spirit not just by Pentecostals but also through the Charismatic movement brought new spiritual vitality to all branches of the church. The twentieth century saw huge expansion and growth of church life. Irrespective of the challenges of the two world wars and subsequent spread of communism throughout the century, the Church grew and spread all over the world with the exception of Europe.

As the Church in the Europe declined Pentecostal expansion everywhere else was phenomenal. Unfortunately, the new denominations became very structured and legalistic with many dividing and splitting forming new ones with disunity becoming the order of the day.

There were very few who had a sense of personal relationship with God as a Father. God the Father was a member of the trinity but not one with whom many people had considered the possibility of having a relationship. There was a huge emphasis on the place of Jesus the Son and nearly all churches taught and considered it essential to have a personal encounter and relationship with Jesus. In many ways, it was a culture of 'Jesus only'.

The Pentecostal style churches particularly emphasised this approach albeit with a strong acknowledgement of the power of the Holy Spirit. There was very little if any mention of the relationship of God the Father to the other members of the Trinity. In many ways, God the Father was seen as the judge and distant sovereign that had been suggested by western Christian thinking since the days of the early Latin fathers. Tertullian in 200 AD had given the language to the Western Church and Augustine defined it and enshrined it into western thinking. This view had become deeply ingrained in medieval church teaching and tradition. Even the reformers of the sixteenth century had not changed this view of God the Father. The idea that God was a relational Father with a love for all humanity was not a feature of any of the reformers with perhaps the exception of Tyndale. William Tyndale in the sixteenth century was one of the great forerunners of this revelation, but his discoveries were probably lost due to his untimely death by martyrdom at the age of 42. Sadly, in the following centuries there were very few who had much understanding of the revelation of God as a Father.

In the 1980's, a slowing in the Charismatic renewal occurred with many churches settling into a gentle charismatic culture rather than a pressing forward into the new things that God had for the church. A huge emphasis on eschatology gripped many evangelicals and Charismatics with a growing expectation of the dawning of the new millennium that would herald an apocalyptic end time event of some kind. The great preoccupation with end time speculation and the hoped for imminent return of Jesus diverted many from what God wanted to reveal to the world. Many were longing for an escape route out of the postmodern world rather than an engagement with the Father to be his sons in the earth.

CHAPTER THIRTEEN

God the Father and Sonship Rediscovered

1900's

In the twentieth century things began to slowly change and the revelation of God as a Father began to be rediscovered. We have seen that there had been some individuals all through history who had touched on the understanding of the importance of the Father's love for his children and the relationship between the Father and the Son. There was a growing understanding that God has been restoring lost truth to the church over the centuries. This process of restoration had been going on since the late middle ages.

There have always been some individuals who have had part of this, but until the invention of the printing press it had been difficult to document. The major breakthrough came with Jan Hus' rediscovery of the truth of justification by faith in Jesus in the fifteenth century.

1400's

1500's

Martin Luther in the sixteenth century had a personal revelation of his own salvation through faith in Christ primarily through studying the Bible in general and Paul's letter to the Romans in particular. As we have seen, Luther's ideas and teaching spread rapidly assisted by the intellectual climate of hunger for knowledge in that century. This was aided by the spread of his writings because of the new technology of printing. All the key leaders and theologians of the sixteenth century had justification by faith as their starting point. The other major factor was the freedom they all espoused of being able to read and interpret the Bible without restriction. Roman Catholics had insisted that only the Church and the Pope could read the Bible and thereby define theology.

As more and more people gained access to the Bible, more forgotten truth was rediscovered and began to be taught. It was a tidal wave of revelation that swept across Europe. One significant factor was the fact that the revelation did not remain the preserve of clergy or scholars but was open to all as people read the Bible for themselves. William Tyndale, as we have seen, was an outstanding example of one whose revelation of God went far deeper than many others in his age.

New thinking was applied to the sacraments. For example, the Roman Catholic sacrament of the Mass was replaced in the Protestant churches with the Lord's Supper at its simplest. The restoration of believer's baptism and the gathered nature of the church was championed by the Anabaptists. By the end of the sixteenth century, the pace of rediscovery of forgotten truth slowed down. The excitement of the new revelation was lost by the second and third generation after the original reformers died. The move of God slowed to a standstill. It was again an example that God has no grandchildren. Each generation needed revelation for itself of the nature and character of God.

We have seen how each new move of God had the tendency to settle and become institutionalised. New truth was enshrined in new denominational structures and forms that quickly atrophied and became restrictive and suspicious of new teaching and revelation. Indeed, they often were in the vanguard of persecuting the next generation who discovered more forgotten truth or thought differently.

Preaching the gospel and teaching of the Bible had been a key practice of the reformers and the new churches that emerged, but as time passed this tended to lack anointing and power. It became enshrined in dull dogmatic statements, prayer books and deadly boring sermons rather than life-giving preaching. As George Whitefield once said, "The reason why congregations have been so dead is because dead men preach to them."

The great commission to take the gospel to all nations was rediscovered by the Moravians in the eighteenth century and brought another major leap forward. Their success was linked to the outpouring of Holy Spirit anointing and power on them. This deeply impacted the Wesleys who carried the revelation forward and brought fresh vitality and life to the moribund church of North America and England.

However, a number of individuals were also edging forward to a new understanding of revelation and truth about God as a Father in the nineteenth century. One important figure in this process was George MacDonald.

GEORGE MACDONALD, *1800's*
A FORERUNNER OF THE REVELATION OF SONSHIP

George MacDonald (1824 – 1905) was a Scottish author, poet, and Christian minister. He was a pioneering figure in the field of fantasy literature and the mentor of fellow writer Lewis Carroll. His writings have been cited as a major literary influence by many notable authors including C.S. Lewis and J.R.R. Tolkien. Introducing MacDonald's *Lilith*, Lewis wrote that he regarded MacDonald as his master. *"Picking up a copy of MacDonald's work Phantastes one day at a train-station bookstall, I began to read. A few hours later,"* said Lewis, *"I knew that I had crossed a great frontier."*

MacDonald's theology has influenced many in the twentieth century as well as C.S. Lewis. MacDonald rejected the doctrine of penal substitutionary atonement, first suggested by Tertullian in 200 AD, which had been picked up and developed by Augustine in 400 AD. This teaching had been addressed by Anslem of Canterbury in the twelfth century and refined by Calvin in the sixteenth century and subsequently, by most reformed Protestant theologians. This doctrine argues that Jesus Christ has taken the place of sinners and is punished by the wrath of God in their place. MacDonald believed that in turn it raised serious questions about the character and nature of God. Instead, he taught that Christ had come to save people from their sins, and not from a Divine penalty for their sins. The problem to MacDonald was not the need to appease a wrathful God but the disease of cosmic evil itself. MacDonald posed the rhetorical question, *"Did he not foil and slay evil by letting all the waves and billows of its horrid sea break upon him, go over him, and die without rebound, spend their rage, fall defeated, and cease?"* His answer was that God made atonement.

MacDonald was convinced that God does not punish except to amend, and that the sole end of his greatest anger is the amelioration of the guilty. To use MacDonald's imagery, the doctor uses fire and steel in certain deep-seated diseases, so God may use hell-fire if necessary to heal the hardened sinner. In his sermon on Justice, MacDonald declared, *"I believe that no hell will be lacking which would help the just mercy of God to redeem his children."* MacDonald posed another rhetorical question in his sermon 'The Consuming Fire', *"When we say that God is Love, do we teach men that their fear of Him is groundless?"* He replied, *"No. As much as they fear will come upon them, possibly far more...The wrath will consume what they call themselves; so that the selves God made shall appear"* (*Unspoken Sermons*).

However, true repentance, in the sense of freely chosen moral growth is essential to this process, and in MacDonald's optimistic view, inevitable for all beings. This has been taken up by his critics to indicate that he was a universalist and therefore not orthodox.

In this theology of divine punishment, MacDonald stands in opposition to Augustine and in agreement with the Greek Fathers, Clement of Alexandria, Origen and Gregory of Nyssa although it is not known whether MacDonald had a working familiarity with them.

In his introduction to *George MacDonald: An Anthology*, C.S. Lewis speaks highly of MacDonald's theology:

> *"This collection, as I have said, was designed not to revive MacDonald's literary reputation but to spread his religious teaching. Hence most of my extracts are taken from the three volumes of Unspoken Sermons. My own debt to this book is almost as great as one man can owe to another: and nearly all serious inquirers to whom I have introduced it acknowledge that it has given them great help—sometimes indispensable help toward the very acceptance of the Christian faith.*
> *...I know hardly any other writer who seems to be closer, or more continually close, to the Spirit of Christ Himself. Hence his Christ-*

like union of tenderness and severity. Nowhere else outside the New Testament have I found terror and comfort so intertwined... In making this collection I was discharging a debt of justice. I have never concealed the fact that I regarded him as my master; indeed I fancy I have never written a book in which I did not quote from him. But it has not seemed to me that those who have received my books kindly take even now sufficient notice of the affiliation. Honesty drives me to emphasize it."

— C.S. Lewis

In MacDonald's book, *Your Life in Christ,* he writes in the chapter 'Who is my Father?' about the Fatherhood of God and how we, as a result, are recognised and placed by him as sons. He says,

"The refusal to look up to God as our father is the one central wrong in the whole human affair. The inability to do so is our one central misery. Whatever helps to clear away any difficulty from our recognition of the Father will more or less eliminate every difficulty in life. "Is God then not my father?" cries the heart of the child. "Do I need to be adopted by him? Adoption! That can never satisfy me. Who is my true father? Am I not his to begin with? Is God not my very own father? Is he my father in word only-by a sort of legal contrivance? Truly, much love may lie in adoption, but if I accept it from anyone, that makes me in reality the actual offspring spring of another! The adoption of God would indeed be a blessed thing if another than he had given me being! But if he gave me being, then it means no reception, but a repudiation. Oh Father, am I not your child?" "No," they say, "but he will adopt you. He will not acknowledge you as his child, but he will call you his child and be a father to you." "Alas!" cries

the child, "if he is not my father, he cannot become my father. A father is a father from the beginning. A primary relation cannot be super induced. The consequence might be small where earthly fatherhood is concerned, but the very origin of my being - alas, alas, if he be only a maker and not a father! Then am I only a machine, and not a child-not a man! If what you say is so, then it is false to say I was created in his image!"

When discussing 'huiothesia' which MacDonald says is inaccurately rendered as 'adoption', he says,

"In the New Testament the word is used only by the apostle Paul. Liddell and Scott give the meaning as "adoption as a son," which is a mere submission to popular theology. They give no reference except to the New Testament. The relation of the word huiothesia to the form which means "taken," or rather, "placed as one's child" is, I presume, the sole ground for the translating of it so. Usage plentiful and invariable, however, could not justify that translation here, in the face of what St. Paul elsewhere shows he means by the word. This Greek word might be variously interpreted-though I can find no use of it earlier than St. Paul. But the English can mean only one thing, and that is not what St. Paul means. "The spirit of adoption" Luther translates "the spirit of a child." Adoption he translates kind-schaft, or childship. Of two things I am sure. First, that by huiothesia St. Paul did not intend adoption. And second, that if the revisers had gone through what I have gone through because of the word, if they had felt it come between God and their hearts as I have felt it, they could not have allowed it to remain in their version. Once more I say, the word used by St. Paul does not imply that God

adopts children that are not his own, but rather that a second
time he fathers his own. A second time they are born-this time
from above. He will make himself tenfold, yea, infinitely their
father. He will have them return into the very bosom whence they
came...and left that they might learn they could live nowhere else.
He will have them one with himself. It was for the sake of this
that, in his Son, he died for them."

We have seen that Macdonald was a major influence on C.S. Lewis who had been converted in the late 1930s while he was an Oxford professor. It is probably true to say that he was to become the most significant Christian writer of the twentieth century in his contribution to pastoral theology, philosophical thought and apologetics. According to his memoir, *Surprised by Joy*, Lewis had been baptised in the Church of Ireland at birth, but fell away from his faith during his adolescence. Owing to the influence of Tolkien and other friends, at about the age of 30, Lewis became a Christian. His conversion had a profound effect on his work, and his wartime radio broadcasts on the subject of Christianity brought him wide acclaim. Later in his life, he married the American writer Joy Gresham, who died of cancer four years after they wed at the age of 45.

Lewis' works have been translated into more than thirty languages and have sold more than a million copies per year, not least the Narnia Chronicles. His influence on many twentieth century writers and theologians is enormous. There are many links from Lewis to those who have rediscovered the revelation of God as Father.

Jack Winter – the First to Speak of God's 'Fatherheart'

In the last two decades of the twentieth century, a new wave of revelation began to build in the church around the world. The key figure in this rediscovery of the truth about the Father's love began with an American, Jack Winter (1931 - 2002). He led a ministry in the USA called Daystar Ministries. Many people were touched by his preaching and ministry and sought him out for personal prayer. Whilst ministering in 1977, he felt God speaking about the need to represent his love to those he was ministering to by holding people in his arms like a child needling to be loved. Initially, he resisted this unconventional ministry activity but after a while obeyed the prompting to do this. As he held people in his arms, he prayed that his arms would represent the Father's arms and those being held would experience the Father loving them. The results were very encouraging with hundreds receiving a powerful encounter of being loved by the Father.

Jack Winter began to teach and minister this truth extensively in spite of resistance and lack of understanding by many. His contacts with Loren Cunningham of Youth With A Mission (YWAM) opened a doorway to the teaching and they took on board much of Winter's teaching through their Discipleship Training Schools. Following an encounter with Jack Winter in 1978, Floyd McClung, a YWAM leader, was deeply touched by this revelation. In 1985, he wrote one of the first books to address the issue entitled *The Father Heart of God*. Other writers at the time included an Anglican charismatic called Tom Smaile who wrote the book *The Forgotten Father*. These and other books began to explore this rediscovered truth of God the Father actively loving his children.

Jack Winter began to impact other significant leaders. In the mid 1980s, he was asked to speak with a young couple at a church in Canada who had experienced a move of God that surprised them. Subsequently, they shut down the move out of inexperience. Jack Winter encouraged them that the move they had experienced was the effect of people being loved by God the Father. This couple was John and Carol Arnott. Jack Winter's ministry to them would bear fruit a decade later in Toronto at the Airport Christian Fellowship.

James and Denise Jordan – and Fatherheart Ministries

A young couple from New Zealand, James and Denise Jordan, encountered the love of the Father through the life and ministry of Jack Winter. The Jordans first met Jack Winter in the mid 1970s, whilst studying at a bible college at Orama on Great Barrier Island, New Zealand. It was a significant visit and led to the Jordans moving to the USA in 1978 with their young family. Unknown to James and Denise, this would be a very pivotal moment in their life and walk with God. During this time, James heard the Lord speak very clearly to him about being 'a Joshua' to Jack and he understood that this would mean becoming to Jack what Joshua was to Moses.

Throughout this time, Jack began to receive a fuller and deeper understanding of the nature of God as the Father.

James Jordan relates that it was not the revelation of the Father that drew him initially to Jack Winter's ministry, but the anointing he perceived the man carried. On their arrival in Minnesota at one of the Daystar centres, James was surprised to find everyone talking about experiencing the Father's love. After some initial resistance, James began to look at some of the reasons why he had struggled to know God as Father. In time, these blockages were removed and he was ministered to by Jack Winter. James tells how Jack asked him if he could be a little boy who needed to be loved. Then Jack put his arms around James and prayed, "Father, let your arms be my arms and will you pour your love into this young man's heart." It was simple and profound. In that moment, James received the love of the Father and as a result, his life was transformed. He has been ministering the revelation of the Father's love ever since. After some time, the Jordans returned to New Zealand and were involved in a number of ministries and churches. Following a time of burn out, they returned to pastoral ministry in Auckland in the early 1990s.

One of the most significant events of the late twentieth century for the Christian world was the outpouring that broke out in Toronto in March 1994 at Toronto Airport Vineyard led by John and Carol Arnott. This outpouring described by the British tabloid press, as the Toronto Blessing, was seen by the Arnotts as the Father's Blessing. Its impact swept around the world and influenced to a lesser or greater extent the whole Christian world. Every nation has been touched. Churches from Roman Catholic to almost every Protestant denomination were impacted. A new grouping of churches and individuals who have embraced the Renewal as it became to be called emerged in 1996. This network is called Partners in Harvest. Many of the churches affiliated initially tried to remain in their original denominations but there has been resistance by some formally cutting edge groupings to distance themselves from the Renewal.

This is true to some extent of the Vineyard movement and New Frontiers. As this renewal continued, there was a growing understanding that the manifestations that accompanied the outpouring were the packaging of a more important truth, namely the revelation of the Father's love for his children. Churches and individuals that did not appreciate this fact have "moved on" and left behind much of the benefits of the blessing, whereas those that have embraced this truth are moving into a deeper understanding of the revelation.

In 1994, Jack Winter urged James Jordan to visit Toronto where he was deeply impacted by the Holy Spirit. In 1997, after a period of great personal challenge, the Jordans left New Zealand again and rejoined Jack Winter in Korea as Fatherheart Ministries. They coined the term 'Fatherheart' which is now used widely by many.

The Jordans travelled extensively for the next six years with Jack and Dorothy Winter. Jack died in 2002 but James continued to minister. At the time of his death, Jack purposefully passed his 'mantel' on to James. Since that time James has continued to grow in this revelation of the Father and on into a deeper awareness of sonship and our inheritance as sons of God.

Other figures who were influenced and helped to spread the revelation included the Roman Catholic priest Henri Nouwen whose book *Return of the Prodigal Son* was published in 1994. Ed Piorek, a Vineyard pastor had a revelation of the Father's Love in 1985. He introduced many within that movement to the revelation. Jack Frost encountered the Father's love after meeting Jack Winter. After a visit to Toronto, he founded Shiloh Place Ministries that carried the revelation and talked about a love reformation. Following his death in 2007, his widow Trisha continued the work of Shiloh Place, leading this ministry.

Many Christian leaders have been deeply impacted by the Toronto experience that has led them into a new appreciation of the Father's love. In 1999, Jack Winter and James and Denise Jordan along with Jack Frost established an annual gathering of ministers and travelling teachers who were spreading the message of the Father's love to the world. These gatherings were called Fatherheart Forums.

James was speaking at Toronto at one of these events and felt God revealing the nature of the orphan spirit to him. This was the first time that this expression was used. He was the first person to begin teaching on this significant topic that is now widely accepted and taught. The substance of the teaching describes the orphan nature of the human race after the fall. Satan was described as the archetypical orphan hearted spirit who dragged humanity into his sphere of influence. The teaching typically recognises the loss of our position as sons of God that we enjoyed before the fall and how we have lived like orphans ever since. Jesus' statement in John 14:18, *"I will not leave you as orphans, I will come to you"* heralds the coming of our return to sonship that Jesus invites us into.

At a Fatherheart Forum in Pasadena California, Denise Jordan first began to teach about the 'Mother' heart of God, a revelation she received about the nurturing and feminine character of God. Those in attendance at that forum were deeply impacted by Denise's teaching and the revelation enshrined within it. Many since have subsequently taken James and Denise's prophetic teachings on and have written and taught similar things. James and Denise have been at the forefront of this ongoing revelation ever since and are widely recognised as the standard bearers of this revelation today.

To enable the spread of this revelation, the Jordans taught at conferences and churches all over the world. However, they did not feel that this gave enough time for people to drink of the full measure of the revelation. They began to see the need for a week long event they called a Fatherheart School in which they could teach the full range of material that had come to embody their message. The first of the Schools, known as A Schools, was held in 2003 with others following in Europe and New Zealand in subsequent years. Around about the same time, they returned to New

Zealand and purchased property in Taupo. They renamed the property The Eden Centre. It came to serve as the main base of Fatherheart Ministries. From this base, they have travelled from and brought people to receive the revelation.

Another person deeply impacted by the revelation brought by the Jordans and Jack Winter is Canadian, Barry Adams. After attending one of the schools, Barry decided to list all the verses in the bible where God the Father describes his loving relationship with his sons. He called this 'The Father's Love Letter'. He loaded it up to his website and within a very short while, the Love Letter had gone viral around the globe with literally millions of hits that led to his server crashing. The letter has now been translated into hundreds of languages all over the world and millions have read it and entered into a new awareness of their position in Christ as sons loved by their heavenly Father.

The Jordans gathered together a group of leaders from within their ministry to a Fatherheart Ministries Leader's Summit in New Zealand in February 2011. During this gathering, it became clear that the revelation of the love of God the Father was not the goal of Fatherheart Ministries. It was rather that the revelation of Father was given in order to lead us back into sonship. Living as sons and daughters to God who is our Father was the revelation of the New Testament Church and was typified by Paul's description of believers as being "in Christ" having received in their hearts the Spirit of Sonship. Fatherheart Ministries has as a result focused on Sonship as a major theme. The second of the weekly Schools known as the B School has as its main focus, living as sons and exploring the nature of our sonship. The A Schools are seen as a doorway into sonship that comes about after a dynamic and real experience of being loved by God the Father. This is not seen as a one off touch, typical of much of the teaching that emerged following the renewal that began in Toronto, rather a continuous living in the day to day reality of being loved as sons by our Father.

When we look back to the New Testament we have seen that this was the central point of the Christian life. The whole gospel was about a Father who wanted to bring man back into the position of sons that he had planned for us before the creation of the world. Jesus came to reveal God as Father to us in order that we could be brought back into that relationship through his redeeming death and the shedding of his blood. To reposition us back into Sonship was the primary reason why Jesus came and this was the first of the major truths of the gospel that was lost by the early Church. Redemption was the process and the end result was our repositioning into sonship. As part of this process of restoring lost truth to the church, which we have seen over the last five hundred years, God has graciously restored this truth to his church in these days.

Since 2011, the major focus of Fatherheart Ministries has been to preach, to teach and to impart this revelation. Increasingly, the method of bringing this revelation is seen as a prophetic teaching for the church today. A number of teams are emerging around the world as A School team leaders have been appointed and released to teach the revelation. By the end of 2015, there will have been over fifty such Schools in the year alone in more than twenty nations. A similar number are planned for 2016. The activity of Fatherheart Ministries continues to be conducted through conferences, church weekends, A and B Schools, Gatherings and the three month school 'Inheriting the Nations School' that has been held annually in New Zealand at Orama on Great Barrier Island. Orama is a place of special significance in the affections of James and Denise as this is where they first met Jack Winter.

Many of James and Denise's teachings and that of their team have been made available as CDs, and as MP3 downloads so much so that the new technology of the twenty-first century like the technology of previous generations has aided the dissemination of the revelation and its teaching around the world. A television station in Southeast Asia has also recorded and broadcast James' teaching at an A School with each programme being translated into Mandarin. In recent years, the writing of books has become a major part of the focus of a number within Fatherheart Ministries, most notably with the publication of James' books on *Sonship*, and *The Ancient Road Rediscovered*, which is a prophetic message to the church of the twenty-first century and *The Forgotten Feminine* by Denise. These books have had a major impact and are being translated into numerous languages. Others within the ministry of Fatherheart Ministries have also published books and there is a growing move to encourage biblical and historical scholarship to undergird the revelation.

There is no sense that we have arrived, rather that we are at the beginning of a new day of revelation. We do not see this as new truth but biblical truth that has been forgotten, overlooked or ignored by many over the centuries. The great truth that we are sons of God through faith in Christ first described by Paul in Galatians is the amazing new ground on which we stand. The knowledge of God as Father has brought us through to this place of sonship that is our inheritance, which we were destined for before the creation of the world.

Father has graciously revealed himself to us afresh in this generation. We have discovered him to be our real Father and we are his sons. But he is not a grandfather and he has no grandsons. Each generation has the potential to lose their connection with him as Father as history sadly bears out. It also has had the potential to soar into greater depths of revelation. It behooves this generation of sons to faithfully preach and teach this prophetic revelation and for the next generation to pick it up for themselves and carry it forward. In their turn I am excited to see what truth they will rediscover that we have not yet seen.

My longing and encouragement to those who love the Father and his Word is that we see beyond what Luther saw, to look beyond what the Anabaptists saw, beyond what the Moravians saw, to go beyond the Pentecostal and Charismatic revivals. Instead my desire is to reopen the bible and read with the eyes of our hearts, without preconception. My challenge is to allow ourselves to have fresh truth revealed to us and be instructed in things that will take us beyond what those who have gone before have seen, taught and received. There will be those who resist and will not want to see. However, there will be those who want to receive more light from the Word. They should have no problem in saying with John Robinson, one of those who had encouraged the leaders of the 1620 Pilgrim Fathers to head off into the unknown,

> *"I charge you before God...that you follow me no further than you have seen me follow the Lord Jesus Christ. If God reveals anything to you by any other instrument of His, be as ready to receive it as you were to receive any truth by my ministry, for I am verily persuaded the Lord hath more truth yet to break forth out of His Holy Word.*

Argentina - Claudio Freidzon 1980's -
France -
Canada - Vineyard / John Arnott

England - William Tyndale, the Wesleys,

Scotland - George MacDonald, 1800's

Other books
by Trevor Galpin

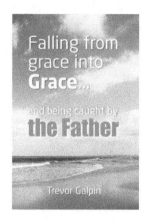 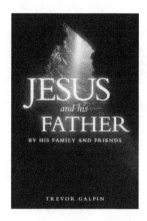

For more information and resources by
Trevor and Linda visit
www.trevorlindafhm.com

Additional resources from Fatherheart Media are available at

www.fatherheart.net/shop - New Zealand
www.fatherheartmedia.com - Europe
www.amazon.com - Paperback & Kindle versions

FATHERHEART MEDIA PO BOX 1039
Taupo 3330,
New Zealand

Visit us at www.fatherheart.net

- Western Religion replaced the doctrine of the Fatherhood of God with His sovereignty. Around 450 AD. P. 105

- Armenia was the 2# nation-state to declare itself Christian, in 301 AD.

- Bible was translated into
  - Latin by Jerome ~ 400 AD
  - Gothic (Germany) ~ 340 AD
    France

- In 430s AD the Gospel reached China by Nestorius p 112

- "Social responsibility", (p. 180) caused by a revival

CPSIA information can be obtained at www.ICGtesting.com
Printed in the USA
LVHW092031190719
624726LV00001B/43/P